31. Buddha Immages

# Thai Ways

Denis Segaller

SILKWORM BOOKS

ISBN 974-9575-73-3

This edition first published in 2005 by

Silkworm Books
6 Sukkasem Road, T. Suthep
Chiang Mai 50200, Thailand
Website: www.silkwormbooks.info
E-mail: info@silkwormbooks.info

Set in 10 pt. Stone Serif by Silk Type

Printed in Thailand by O. S. Printing House, Bangkok

10 9 8 7 6 5 4 3 2 1

# Preface

This book is dedicated to my wife Laddawan, without whom at least half the articles in it would never have been written; to Anussorn, without whom at least the other half would never have been written; and to Juli, who kept on saying she enjoyed reading them when they originally appeared as a regular weekly column in the *Bangkok World*, the former afternoon tabloid companion to the *Bangkok Post*.

My sincere thanks also go (in retrospect) to the *Bangkok World* for running the articles in the first place; to The Post Publishing Company Limited, who kindly agreed to their being reprinted in book form; to Thai Airways International, who originally sponsored the publishing of the book during its first two printings, and especially to Chitdee Rangavara and Roy Howard, both then working with Thai Airways, as well as to Mom Rachawongse Putrie Viravaidya, for their encouragement and help; and to all the many other friends and former colleagues who helped me with ideas for articles and with problems of translation from Thai.

When going through the wealth of material – the weekly "Thai Ways" column ran continuously from 1975–1985 – I found it difficult to be 100 percent logical about its classification and presentation as a book. What is the difference between a festival and a ceremony? Or between a ceremony and a custom? Or a custom and a belief? The divisions are bound to be blurred, and details in the various sections of the book often overlap. Many of these repetitions have been deliberately retained from the original articles. Not only do they help to make each section more or less complete in itself, but perhaps, too, they will help to convey a feeling of the intricate network of ideas and customs that make up the life and culture of Thailand.

In the Second Edition, published in 1989 (the seventh or eigth impression, if memory serves), I made a few minor alterations in the text.

In this Third Edition, I have revised the text to correct various inaccuracies brought about by the passage of time. However, the majority of the text remains as true today as when it was first written between 1975–79.


Denis Segaller
Pathum Thani, August 1993

# A Note on Thai Words

The Thai language has its own beautiful, decorative, and historically rich script which carries overtones of the ancient Sanskrit, Pali, Mon, and Khmer languages. The spelling of all Thai words in Thai script is precise and logical. However, when "transliterated" or "Romanized" into the Western "ABC" alphabet, there are in practice no hard and fast rules (although Thailand's Royal Institute has laid down an official system showing which Thai letters correspond to which Western ones). This imprecision in practice can be illustrated by a little anecdote.

Soon after I first arrived in Thailand, I was talking on the phone with a Thai friend, who said "You must contact Mr. "X" (telling me a Thai name). "How do you spell that?" I asked. "Well," he answered, "let's see; how would you like to spell it?"

In fact, the same Thai name is often spelt in a variety of ways in the Western alphabet, as mentioned briefly in Chapter 9. It is all rather arbitrary and a matter of personal choice.

D.S.

Publisher's note: This edition follows the Royal Institute system of Romanization, with the exception of personal names, and a few other terms, as noted.

# Contents

CONTENTS

# Chapter One

# Royalty and Nobility

## Ranks and Titles in Thailand

The system of ranks and titles in Thailand today, from Their Majesties the King and Queen downwards through the nobility to commoners, is fairly complex and has an interesting history. Today's system is actually far simpler than those of earlier times. It is, in fact, derived from the earlier systems, but not until the publication in 1878 of an essay by King Chulalongkorn (Rama V) was a complete understanding of the system as it existed during his reign made possible.

Professor Robert B. Jones of Cornell University's Department of Asian Studies has translated King Chulalongkorn's essay under the title *Thai Titles and Ranks, Including a Translation of Traditions of Royal Lineage in Siam, by King Chulalongkorn.* Here are some of the colorful details from this interesting book which throw light on the pomp and ceremony of Thailand's past.

The Royal Decree known as *kotmonthianban* ("for the preservation of the King's household"), otherwise known as the Palatine Law or Palace Regulations, was promulgated during the reign of Somdet (His Majesty) Phra Ramathibodi I, the founder of Ayutthaya, in A.D. 1358. Besides setting out the dignity and honor of the King, princes, government officials, and regulations concerning the deportment of the latter to ensure they did not commit offences towards the King, the Law divided the King's children into four ranks according to the status of the mother. Each rank had to defer to those of higher rank – that is, to walk behind them and to salute them.

Two of the four princely ranks were entitled to be governors of provincial towns; such ranks were known as *Chao Fa*, the same title used for Their Majesties' children today. The name literally means "Lord of Heaven." The Palatine Law says that a *Chao Fa* was traditionally anointed with water from the same bowl used for anointing the King at his coronation. Soon after a *Chao Fa's* birth, special lullabies were sung with words such as "you have come to rule the country to protect the Royal Family and the people." Even the infant *Chao Fa's* nurses held special titles. As the child grew older special rites were held, of which cutting the topknot was perhaps the most elaborate.

A *Chao Fa* had a "dignity" or "status" much higher than that of other princes. This "diginity" is known in Thai as *sakdina*, and I'm going to hazard a guess that this can be translated as "field status" because of its very precise and practical numerical meaning: It denoted the maximum number of *rai*\* of land that a person was permitted to own. For instance, a *Chao Fa* who was a king's younger brother had a "dignity" of 20,000; a king's son had 15,000; and if either of these princes were appointed Deputy King, his "dignity" rose to 100,000. Thus the number of units depended on rank by birth and also rank conferred subsequently by the King. Government officials were also allowed to possess land, and thus qualified for "dignity" too.

\*1 *rai* = 0.395 acres; 6.25 *rai* = 1 hectare

In passing, it may be noted that a *Chao Fa*'s betel tray and spittoon – both of them symbols of rank – were of gold with blue enamel, unlike those of other princes, which were of plain gold. When a *Chao Fa* died, a mourning woman wailed a special mourning song for him, and a funeral pyre was built in the centre of the city.

During the more than three-hundred-year period between the later Ayutthaya Period and the Bangkok of King Chulalongkorn's day, seven classes of persons were qualified to hold the rank of *Chao Fa*. Even when the King's essay was written, the ways in which a person could become a *Chao Fa* were still rather complex.

Today it is sufficient to know that Their Majesties the King and Queen are *ipso facto* the heads of Thailand's nobility and aristocracy, and that their children are still known as *Chao Fa* in normal parlance: *Chao Fa Chai* ("male") in the case of His Royal Highness Crown Prince Vajiralongkorn, and *Chao Fa Ying* ("female") for Their Royal Highnesses Princess Maha Chakri Sirindhorn and Princess Chulabhorn.

The child of a male *Chao Fa* is known nowadays as *Phra-ong Chao* (the English title is again His or Her Royal Highness). If a female *Phra-ong Chao* marries a commoner, she forfeits her rank and official title. The child of a male *Phra-ong Chao* is a *Mom Chao* (in English, His or Her Serene Highness). Again, if a female *Mom Chao* marries a commoner, she forfeits her title and becomes known informally as *Than Ying*, followed by her personal name. These three ranks – *Chao Fa*, *Phra-ong Chao*, and *Mom Chao* – constitute the nobility. They must be addressed in *rachasap* – royal language – by one another and by commoners.

Hereditary titles below that of *Mom Chao* are commoners. The child of a male *Mom Chao* is a *Mom Rachawongse*. If male, he is also known casually as *Khunchai*; if female, she is known as *Khunying*. The latter should not be confused with the conferred title of the same name given in recognition of good work done for the State. If a female *Mom Rachawong* marries a commoner, she retains her *Mom Rachawong* title, but assumes her husband's surname.

The child of a male *Mom Rachawong* is a *Mom Luang*. The male or female child of a *Mom Luang* has no title, but puts "*Na Ayutthaya*" after his or her surname. If male, his wife is also entitled to this suffix, even if she is a commoner. A female child of a *Mom Luang*, however, forfeits the *Na Ayutthaya* when she marries and takes her husband's surname.

In the past, the earlier kings conferred ranks on commoners in the form of life peerages, but this custom was discontinued after the reign of King Vajiravudh (Rama VI). A few such persons are still living; these conferred titles were *Somdet Chaophya, Chaophya, Phya, Phra, Luang,* and *Khun*.

## King Mongkut of Siam*

King Mongkut (Rama IV), who reigned from 1851 to 1868, was the first Asian monarch to speak, read, and write fluent English. This feat was all the more remarkable because at that time there was no Siamese-English dictionary. He therefore had to translate first from Siamese into ancient Pali, and then search for an English equivalent in a vast Pali-English dictionary. To be on the safe side, he often inserted

---

*The writer is indebted for the material in this section to two books: *Mongkut the King of Siam* by Abbot Low Moffat, Cornell University Press; and *The Dynastic Chronicles, Bangkok Era, the Fourth Reign* translated by Chadin [Kanchanavanit] Flood, Centre for East Asian Cultural Studies, Tokyo.

two or more alternatives from the English words listed, and this gave his writings a distinctly individual flavor. For instance, in letter to the Governor of Penang dated April 21, 1851, announcing his accession to the throne of Siam, he wrote:

> Whereas His Majesty the late King was expired and demised on the 2nd instant, on next day of which day I was elected and entered into this place where I am living happily with great business or affair of presiding over whole kingdom, but my enthronement or exaltation will be on 15th May for waiting of the greatest preparation the ceremony of my crowning . . .

*Mongkut* is the Thai word for "crown," and before he became king he was known as *"Chao Fa* Mongkut," or "the High Prince of the Crown" – that is, "His Royal Highness the Crown Prince." After his accession he was known in Thai as *Phra Chom Klao*, which means roughly "Most Great King Top of the Head," implying the traditional reverence with which the head, and especially the top of the head, has always been regarded by the Thai people. But to foreigners he has always remained "King Mongkut."

He was a brilliant scholar, a humanitarian, and one of the nineteenth century's greatest Asian statesmen. Born in 1804, King Mongkut was brought up in the full royal manner of one born to rule. In accordance with royal custom, he became a Buddhist novice for seven months at the age of fourteen. When he was twenty and already the father of two children, he again entered the monkhood, this time as a full monk, and, as fate eventually decreed, for twenty-seven years. It was an experience which would gradually shape his whole attitude towards his people and nation when he later became king. He exchanged the pomp and luxury of the royal court for the humble, self-denying life of the orange robes – a true democracy under the Buddhist discipline.

During those twenty-seven years, King Mongkut wrought great changes in the understanding and practice of Buddhism in Siam, bringing back a knowledge of the Buddha's teachings that had become largely lost over the centuries. He also had the leisure and opportunity to put his natural intellect to work. He mastered the Pali language and learnt Sanskrit as well as several other Asian languages, and met various Western scholars through whom he learnt Latin and English. Later, as king, he even wrote an English grammar. He also studied the sciences, particularly astronomy, at which he became expert. He read English books and magazines, and from American missionaries he learnt about the West, its history and systems of government.

But it was perhaps his contact with ordinary folk, with his fellow countrymen and women, during his years in the monkhood which influenced Mongkut most. Not only did he meet them on his daily alms-round, he made many pilgrimages throughout the country. Walking barefoot from village to village, he mixed intimately with the people and learnt their needs, sufferings, and aspirations. On one such pilgrimage in 1833 he discovered among the ruins of the old capital of Sukthothai the now famous stone pillar of King Ramkhamhaeng bearing the first known writing in the Thai alphabet.

After his accession to the throne at the age of forty-seven, King Mongkut's two basic aims were to better the lot of his people and to preserve Siam's independence from foreign powers. He was wise enough and shrewd enough to realise that this latter aim meant not only careful diplomacy, a skilful balancing act between the British and the French, but also the modernization of Siam itself. All his efforts as king were devoted towards these goals and he was strikingly successful. He once expressed Siam's problem in these words:

> Being, as we are now, surrounded by powerful nations, what can a small nation like us do? . . . The only weapons of real use to us will be our mouths and our hearts, constituted so as to be full of sense and wisdom for the better protection of ourselves.

The highlight of King Mongkut's foreign diplomacy and statesmanship was perhaps the signing in 1855 of a treaty with Great Britain, which completely changed Siam's relations with the Western world. It opened the country to foreign trade and ensured the welfare of Westerners living in Siam, thus gaining the recognition and respect of Europe and the United States for Siam as a sovereign and independent country. A member of the British mission who signed the treaty wrote: "The King is really an enlightened man. . . . He entered into the Treaty well aware of its force and meaning, and is determined to execute faithfully all his engagements, which are certainly of the most liberal nature."

King Mongkut's reforms and acts of humanity towards his subjects were many. He reinstituted the ancient Siamese right of the common people to petition the King directly in case of injustice, and created new laws to improve the rights of women and children. "It appears the parents sell the daughter as if she were to enter a mousetrap," he wrote. "Parents are not owners of their children in the same way as owners of cattle and elephants may put a price on them and sell them. Therefore, the rule of free will must be made applicable to prevent havoc being wrought on women sold into bondage by their parents." Thus he took the first steps towards the abolition of slavery in Siam.

Although a devout Buddhist, King Mongkut upheld tolerance for other religions, as his predecessors had done. "Never," he wrote, "in the long and continuous history of Siam had any of its kings ever made himself an enemy of any religious faith in this Kingdom . . . This tradition breathes a spirit of happy tolerance among the people of the Kingdom."

On a more down-to-earth matter, he wrote: "It is said that the dwellers in the Divine City (Bangkok) do dishonor to their own city by throwing carcasses of dead animals into the river and canals, where they float up and down in great abomination . . . Wherefore, His Majesty is graciously pleased to advise that under no circumstances whatever should any person allow himself to throw a dead dog, cat, or the carcass of any other animal into the river or canal."

This concern over pollution was matched by an equal preoccupation with improving transport. King Mongkut ordered the construction of many new waterways and roads. *The Dynastic Chronicles, Bangkok Era, the Fourth Reign* (see note at end of this section) describes one highly practical method used to enlarge a canal in a provincial town: "The shortcut canal was found to be too shallow . . . The people who were hired to re-dig it chased buffaloes down into the canal, and by having the buffaloes walk over the entire way, the bottom of the canal sunk down, becoming deeper and wider."

*The Dynastic Chronicles* provide many revealing glimpses of King Mongkut's compassion, both for his fellow humans and for animals. "The King remarked that he had never visited the cities of Ratchaburi and Kanchanaburi . . . He wished to find out if the government officials of those cities had been caring for the people, and to see whether the people were happy or troubled in any way. . . . All along the route, the people brought out their children to pay their respects to the King. They lined both sides of the route, and even presented to the King things they had obtained from the forests... The King talked to them and gave money to those that were old or disabled. . . . He inquired of them as to their well-being . . ." The parallel with the present King of Thailand, His Majesty King Bhumibol, is striking.

When King Mongkut's sixtieth birthday was to be celebrated, he knew that thousands upon thousands of people would be offering food to the monks, and would buy large amounts of fresh meat and fish to do so. Realizing that this would cost the lives of many animals, he gave orders that no one was to buy fresh meat or fish for almsgiving, but instead they must use dry, salted meat and fish.

During his reign King Mongkut built five new temples and restored another thirty-five. Among them was the magnificent Phra Pathom *Chedi* at Nakhon Pathom near Bangkok, believed to be the place where Buddhism was first introduced into Thailand, and today the tallest Buddhist pagoda in Southeast Asia. (See Chapter 10.)

A young present-day Thai scholar who has read King Mongkut's diaries, published in Thai but unfortunately not in English, said: "He was a very good and wise person who was struggling between the old ways and the new modernization offered by the West. He had a keen, shrewd and above all an analytical mind. He was an innovator ahead of his time. Today, modern climatologists are just beginning to study King Mongkut's diaries – based on his meticulously accurate meteorological observations taken with the barometer sent him as a gift by Britain's Queen Victoria." In a rather lighter vein, the same young lady scholar continues:

9

"He also spoke straight to the point and scientifically. He wrote in his diary: 'Thai people like to eat spicy food because they believe it absorbs wind in the belly. This is nonsense.'"

After seventeen years on the throne, King Mongkut traveled in 1868 to Prachuap Khiri Khan in the south of Thailand with a large entourage, including many Western scientists, to view the total eclipse of the sun which he himself had predicted correctly and with great accuracy. While there he caught "jungle fever" – malaria – and he died shortly after his return to Bangkok. On his deathbed, he commanded: "When I am no more, go on with our good work in the interest of the people. Be just to them, and foremost, you must see that their petitions are received and attended to . . ."

King Mongkut brought his country out of the past into the modern era, enabling Siam to take its place among the nations of the world. He did this by a skilful adaptation of Siam's culture and ideas so as to harmonize with those of the West; and it was accomplished without strife, in a reign of peace. Today, two of his observatories – at the old summer palaces of Bang Pa-in and at Phetchaburi – where he sat and watched the stars may be visited. The latter is situated on a hilltop with breathtaking views, and contains many interesting mementoes of this wise and remarkable King.

## *Rachasap* – The Royal Language

When speaking to or about royalty, a special form of Thai is used, known as *rachasap*: "The Royal Language." The first part of this word *rachasap* comes from the ancient Sanskrit word *raj*, meaning "great, powerful, a ruler." The word as a whole means literally "the royal vocabulary." *Rachasap* today forms a fundamental part of Thai culture and tradition – every bit as much as during its earliest known origins in the Sukhothai period some seven hundred years ago – and its qualities and meaning have changed very little since then. Every Thai knows about *rachasap*, though comparatively few are able to speak it correctly. But it can be heard almost every day spoken on TV and the radio, whenever there is a news item or programme about Their Majesties or other members of the Royal Family.

During the Sukhothai period, when the earliest records of *rachasap* are found, Thailand's culture was strongly influenced by its rich, powerful, and highly civilized neighbor, Cambodia. As a result, many *rachasap* words are of Khmer (Cambodian) origin. But many other of its words have come into *rachasap* from Pali and Sanskrit through the Buddhist religion.

Many of the words used in speaking *rachasap* are the same as in ordinary spoken Thai. For instance, when talking with Their Majesties, a Thai uses the ordinary word for table. But not for "chair," unless it is the chair in which he or she (the speaker) is sitting, in which case he calls it by its ordinary name, *kao-i*. But in referring to the chair in which His or Her Majesty is sitting, the speaker must use the *rachasap* form, *phra-kao-i*.

This example illustrates the way in which many *rachasap* nouns are formed: Simply by adding the prefix *phra-*. This is spelt (in Thai characters) the same way as the word for "a monk." It is of Sanskrit origin and is defined by the dictionary as being "prefixed to names of kings, objects associated with royalty, gods, and other objects of worship." Other examples of its use in *rachasap* are *phra-kon* (a king's hands); *phra-net* (his eyes); and *phra-thi* (his bed).

*Phra-* is also combined with *racha* to mean "royal," as in *phra-racha-krasae* (a royal remark or command); *phra-rachadamri* (the King's opinion); *phra-racha-wang* (a royal palace); and *pleng phra-racha-niphon* (songs composed by the King).

A rather less common *rachasap* prefix for nouns is *chalong*. This is used for personal articles. *Chalong-phrabat* (the King's footwear) and *chalong-phra-hat* (royal table cutlery) are two examples.

The other very common *rachasap* prefix is *song*. This is used to form verbs. Placed in front of a *rachasap* noun or an ordinary noun, *song-* converts it into a *rachasap* verb, referring to an action by Their Majesties the King or Queen: *Song-phra-racha-damri* (to be of the opinion); *song-ma* (to ride on horseback); *song-ruea-bai* (to go sailing); *song-*piano and *song-*saxophone (to play the piano and saxophone, respectively). *Song-* is also used in front of certain ordinary verbs, such as *song-sap* (to know) and *song-yin-di* (to be glad). And there are special *rachasap* verbs not used in ordinary Thai, such as *sadet* (to make a journey) and *sawoei* (to eat).

All these verbs are used only when it is a member of the Royal Family who is the subject of the sentence – that is, who is performing the action in question. If you're watching TV or listening to the radio during a description of any royal activity or function, the sounds that you'll notice most often are those of the two common *rachasap* prefixes mentioned above: *phra-* and *song-*.

But the historical and cultural roots of *rachasap* are at their most striking in the forms used for the personal pronouns corresponding to "I," "Your Majesty," and "His or Her Majesty." A Thai man or woman addressing either of Their Majesties expresses "I" by *kha-phra-phutthachao*, literally "slave of the Lord Buddha."

The form corresponding to "Your Majesty" in the case of the King is even longer. The sovereign has always been considered as standing so high above others that he cannot be addressed directly. Even his feet are above the eye-level of ordinary people. So instead of addressing the monarch directly, they must address the dust beneath the soles of his feet. In place of "Your Majesty" they say *tai fa la-ong thuli phra bat*: Literally "under soles, coarse visible dust, fine invisible dust, gracious feet." The number of words used to express "Your Royal Highness," "Your Highness," "Your Excellency," and so on becomes progressively less in descending order of rank.

The third-person pronoun is rather simpler. When Thai people talk among themselves about members of the Royal Family, the *rachasap* word *phra-ong-than* should strictly be used. But among one's family and friends most people refer to His Majesty the King as *Nai Luang* and Her Majesty the Queen as *Somdet*. Many people, however, refer to His Majesty as *phrachao-yu-hua*: "The Lord Buddha in my head" or "the one I worship."

An amusing side-effect of *rachasap* occurred during Her Royal Highness Princess Maha Chakri Sirindhorn's first term at Chulalongkorn University. Her classmates, under the impression that she must be spoken to only in *rachasap*, tripped over themselves verbally in trying to do so. Some of them became so confused that they even started addressing each other in *rachasap*! But the charming and modest Princess soon put everyone at their ease, saying, "You don't have to use *rachasap* when we chat together here, you know."

Perhaps the most eloquent and beautiful example of *rachasap* as a living language, heard and sung by millions daily, is the royal anthem, *Sansoen Phra Barami*, or "Praise to the Royal Grandeur." Following are the words in Thai, together with an English translation which, it is hoped, preserves the spirit of the original.

*Khawora phutha chao*
I, slave of the Lord Buddha,

*ao mano lae sira kran*
prostrate my heart and head

*nop Phraphumiban*
to pay homage and give great

*bunya direk*
blessings to the Protector of the Land

*ek baromma chakarin*
one of the great Chakri Dynasty

*phra sayamin*
Head of the Thai people

*phra yodsa ying yong*
supreme in rank

*yen sira phro phra boriban*
I drew comfort from your protection

*phon phra khun tha raksa*
Because of your gracious care

*puang pracha pen suksan*
all the people are happy and peaceful,

*kho bandan*
We pray

*tha prasong dai*
That whatever you wish for

*chong sarit dang wang wora haruethai*
fate will grant you according to your heart's desire, to bring you prosperity.

*ducha thawai chai chaiyo.*
We salute you!

# Chapter Two

# Festivals

## *Loi Krathong*

The latter part of October and the first three weeks of November form the twelfth lunar month, called in Thai *duean sip-song*. This time of year is sometimes called *na nam* – the high-water season, when there is "water, water everywhere." In some years the lower-lying parts of Bangkok are flooded even on sunny days with blue skies. It is the season when, in Thai words, *nam ko nong tem taling*, or when the water overflows the banks of rivers and canals, or *khlong* as they are known in Thai.

In rural Thailand at this time of year houses are surrounded by canal-jars brimful with water – as many as ten or even twenty jars round each house. Some are filled with rainwater, others with less pure water ladled out painstakingly from the canals nearby. The rainwater will be used for drinking and the canal water for cooking during the dry and hot months to come. As for taking a bath, well, the canal itself provides a very convenient bathroom . . .

The full-moon day of the twelfth lunar month is *Loi Krathong* Day, one of Thailand's most popular and delightful yearly festivals. This is the day on which all this great mass of overflowing water is saluted and celebrated by floating the delicate, dainty, and typically Thai creations called *krathong* on any and every stretch of water in the kingdom.

From dawn to midnight, the radio will be playing the *Loi Krathong* song:

> *"Wan phen duean sipsong,*
> *nam ko nong tem taling*
> *rao thang lai, chai ying*
> *sanuk kan ching wan loi krathong!*
> *loi, loi krathong, loi, loi krathong,*
> *loi krathong kan laeo kho cheon nong kaeo*
> *ok ma ramwong:*
> *ramwong wan loi krathong,*
> *ramwong wan loi krathong!*
> *bun cha song hai rao suk chai,*
> *bun cha song hai rao suk chai!"*

If you can't sing that in Thai, you might care to try my English translation. Admittedly it is a bit rough, but with a little effort you can just about make the words fit the tuneful Thai melody:

> "On twelfth-month full-moon,
> water overflows the canal:
> all of us, men and women
> have lots of fun on *Loi Krathong*!
> *Loi,* by *krathong; loi,* by *krathong,*
> when we've floated our *krathong*s,
> we ask the girls to dance *ramwong*;
> *ramwong* on *Loi Krathong* Day,
> *ramwong* on *Loi Krathong* Day!
> Good deeds will bring us happiness,

good deeds will bring us happiness!"
(Well, at least you might try singing it in the bath –
  a very appropriate place, surely.)

There is always enough water around for everyone to *loi*, or float, his or her *krathong*. After dark every stretch of water in Thailand glitters with the bobbing lights of thousands of candles inside the beautiful little banana-leaf baskets.

In Thai folklore, five goddesses personify the five material elements: *Mae Phra* Thoranee, or Mother Earth; *Mae Phra* Phai, goddess of the wind; *Mae Phra* Phloeng, goddess of fire; *Mae* Phosop, goddess of grain or food; and *Mae* Khongkha or Mother Water. ("Khongkha" really means the Ganges, but has come to mean water in general.) *Loi Krathong* is the annual festival of thanksgiving to *Mae* Khongkha for her bounty in providing water not only for drinking and washing, but for the essential means of livelihood of most Thais: Agriculture, fishing, and transport by river and canal. At the same time, *Loi Krathong* is a request for *Mae* Khongkha's forgiveness for having used and polluted the water. Many people also believe that as their *krathong* floats away, the water washes away their sins of the past year.

*Loi Krathong* is inseparable in Thai people's minds from the legend of a beautiful and talented lady called Nang Nopphamat (pronounced "Noppamaht"), the daughter of a learned Brahmin priest at the court of King Maha Thammaracha during the Sukhothai Dynasty some seven hundred years ago. Wanting to honour *Mae* Khongkha in her own Brahmin fashion, and being highly skilled and inventive, Nang Nopphamat made the very first *krathong* in the form in which we know it today, shaped like a large and exquisite lotus flower. She presented it to the King, who accepted it, lit the candle inside it and launched it on the water.

Every year there are Nang Nopphamat parades through-out Thailand. At Chulalongkorn University every faculty stages a procession with a float carrying its own "Nang Nopphamat" chosen from the faculty's most beautiful girl students. If you are in the vicinity of Phya Thai Road after dark, it is well worth dropping in to the campus for a look.

But then, you will probably be having your own *Loi Krathong* ceremony. All the markets and many shops have *krathong* for sale. After dark, take your *krathong* and a box of matches to the nearest stretch of water, light the candle and joss-sticks, float your *krathong* on the water, *wai* with the palms of your hands joined, and make a wish. If the candle is still burning as the *krathong* floats out of sight, this will bring you good luck in the coming year. Here's wishing you a very happy *Loi Krathong*!

## Songkran

*Songkran* is the traditional Thai New Year. It marks the time when the Sun passes from the zodiac sign of Aries into that of Taurus and is celebrated every year on April 13 or 14. In fact, *Songkran*, which once was not only the traditional but also the official Thai New Year, spreads over three days from the thirteenth to the fifteenth, and this has always been a happy festival-time for one and all.

In the provinces, it remains an occasion for young men and girls to meet. The season is just right for leisurely court-ing, with the rice harvesting finished and the planting of the new crop not yet begun. In the North, around Chiang Mai, sand is taken into temple compounds at this time. It is believed that this will bring good health and prosperity, and that the more sand one takes into the compound, the better. The sand is built into miniature *chedi,* or pagodas, which are then garlanded with flowers – another good chance for boys and girls to meet.

*Songkran* Day begins with early morning merit-making: Offering food to monks, releasing caged birds into the air and fish into rivers and streams, and paying homage to one's ancestors. *Songkran* has always been associated with water, and respects are paid to elder relatives and friends by pouring scented water over the palms of their hands while uttering a wish of blessing.

This is also the time for a general spring-cleaning, including washing the household Buddha images with scented water. To give the public a chance to venerate the Buddha, the famous Phra Phuttha Sihing image is brought out from its home in the National Museum on this one day in the year and paraded through the streets so the crowds may reverently throw scented water over it. And besides these more reverential forms of paying respect, water is thrown rather less ceremoniously by, and at, all and sundry.

I remember one occasion many years ago when I went with another Englishman to see the *Songkran* celebrations at Phra Pradaeng, south of Thonburi. This is a Mon community, which may be the reason why *Songkran* is celebrated a few days later than in Bangkok. We had been told that the *Songkran* procession at Phra Pradaeng was particularly fine, with lots of beautiful Miss Songkrans, and my friend had borrowed an 8-mm cine-camera for the occasion.

It was lucky that the camera was in a waterproof plastic bag – no sooner had we got out of the car than we were soaked to the skin. Some enthusiastic members of the local population hurled water-filled plastic bags at us, which burst upon impact; others smilingly drenched us with buckets of water, and one cheerful youngster even turned a hose on us. And they kept it up; the barrage of water was continuous and relentless.

When we wiped the water from our eyes so that we could at least see, we sought shelter. We could see a corner noodleshop which looked like a reasonably safe vantage-point. But unfortunately, it was about a hundred yards from where we had parked the car. We decided to make a dash for it.

With my friend protecting the wretched and unwanted cine-camera against his person as best he could, we ran the gauntlet of truckloads of cheering citizenry who pelted us with more water-bombs until we reached the sanctuary of the noodle-shop. Here, we stood cautiously in the doorway, ducking quickly inside each time another truckload armed with water-bombs passed by, hoping to see the procession.

As time dragged on we began to lose hope. Neither of us could speak much Thai, and we certainly did not know the word for "procession." Maybe it would not pass that way after all.

Then, after nearly two hours, our patience was rewarded. A magnificent procession with floats bearing seven groups of really lovely girls in wonderful costumes drove slowly past. There was a band, the clash of drums, and a great noise of rhythmic hand-clapping. The sight was well worth the waiting – and the wetting! Too bad my friend did not get any movie shots, though.

After that the supply of local drenching-water seemed to dry up. We made our way damply homewards.

# Chapter Three

# Ceremonies

## The Thai Wedding Ceremony

Some years ago my maid invited me to her niece's wedding. I accepted with real pleasure, because although I had been to several afternoon water-pouring wedding ceremonies, this was my first invitation to the early-morning blessing ceremony at the house of the bride-to-be's family.

I cannot remember what lunar month it was, but it must have been an even-numbered one. Even-numbered lunar months are favored for weddings in Thailand for a very simple, logical reason: a wedding involves two people, so the month in which it takes place should fittingly be a multiple of two: The second, fourth, sixth, or eighth lunar month. But is should not be the tenth or twelfth. Instead, the ninth month, because the number nine is associated in Thailand with progress and prosperity. This is only one of the many traditions associated with weddings in Thailand, whether among the humble folk of the countryside, or the highest in the land.

Anyway, I arrived at the modest house in its tiny compound in an obscure lane at about seven a.m. I was shown into the "best room," where nine monks were seated on cushions in a wide semi-circle (again, the number nine is for the same reason). Inside the semi-circle knelt the bride and groom. Each wore a crown of looped white yarn called a *mongkhon*. The two *mongkhon* were joined together to symbolize matrimonial unity.

The bride was only a little slip of a thing, but she looked absolutely stunning in her wedding hairdo and make-up. The groom was dressed quietly in a dark, Western-style suit. They both knelt with palms joined in salutation, clasping burning joss-sticks. At the back of the room sat about thirty relatives and friends.

The monks held a white thread passing from hand to hand round the semi-circle and out through the window so that it encircled the entire compound. This was the *sai sin*, the sacred cord whose purpose is to keep away evil spirits and protect everyone inside it. The *sai sin* forms an essential part of every Buddhist ceremony.

The senior monk intoned a long blessing, interspersed with deep, loud chanting by the whole group of monks in unison. This went on for about half an hour. The purpose of this early morning ceremony was to bless everything and everyone connected with the wedding. The senior monk then sprinkled holy water over the couple with a sprig of *mayom*, a local shrub sometimes known as a Chinese gooseberry. This brought the ceremony to an end.

Then began the merit-making – the giving of food to the nine monks. Everyone, monks and guests, went out into the tiny backyard, where a tremendous bustling business of ladling out dish after dish of steaming rice, meat, and vegetables started. To my amazement and embarrassment I discovered my maid had somehow found time to set a table aside with my usual very English breakfast of orange juice, poached eggs, toast and coffee . . .

After the meal was over, the monks left and the guests filed out in a procession led by the bride and groom, flanked by two "best men," each carrying a tall leafy bamboo branch about twenty feet high, which formed a kind of archway.

At five o'clock that evening I went to the other main part of the ceremony, known as *rot nam*, or lustral water-pouring. Unlike the early-morning Buddhist ceremony, the pouring of lustral water over the couple's hands is Brahmin in origin. On this particular occasion a large assembly room had been hired. Here all the guests sat in neat rows of chairs, and the young couple again knelt side by side on a small dais, their two heads joined by the white yarn linking the *mongkhon* on the head of each. Their foreheads were anointed as a blessing by the most senior guest with three white dots from a powder made and blessed by the monks that morning. The couple's forearms rested on a narrow ornamental table and their hands hung downwards, palms joined. Bridesmaids in beautiful pink traditional Thai costumes stood in the background.

Slowly a procession formed for the water-pouring. Led by senior members and friends of both families, everyone in turn filed past the kneeling couple. Each guest poured lustral water from a conch shell over the hands of bride and groom, murmuring a wish for lifelong happiness.

In a water-pouring ceremony, the water must be collected in some sort of vessel, or it would soon flood the floor! For this purpose there is another charming Brahmin custom: The use of ornate bowls called *khan* standing on small pedestals called *phan*. The two sets of *khan* and *phan* for collecting the water poured over the couple's hands are filled with flower petals in elaborate patterns, an art in which Thai women excel. The flowers used are the lotus, another flower called "the flower whose petals never fall off" or "the ever-lasting flower," which symbolizes that the happy union will last forever, and a third, the "love flower."

After the last guest had poured the water, a delightful informal party began – plenty of good Thai food and drink, and Thai and Western music and dancing well into the night.

Unlike wedding ceremonies in present-day Bangkok, rural ceremonies usually last two or three days. During this time it is forbidden for the groom to touch the bride. On the first day of the ceremony, the groom goes to the bride's house in a procession with gifts. Near the destination, children form "toll-gates," standing in pairs to bar the way. At the first gate, which is usually just a piece of string stretched between the two children, the leader of the procession asks: "What gate is this?" "The silver gate!" comes the reply. "How much must we pay to go through?" "Twenty baht." (About one U.S. dollar.)

A bit further on there is another "gate," this time real silver, perhaps a borrowed woman's belt. The price here may be fifty baht. Passing the last "golden gate," a gold chain or necklace, may cost one hundred baht, or perhaps even more in these inflationary times.

Thai weddings, one way and another, are expensive affairs – and unlike in the West, it is the bridegroom's family who pays!

## Calling Blessings on a New House

I have been investigating the Thai ceremony of blessing a new house. I had always believed that this was a Buddhist ceremony, because one can sometimes see the main post of a house-to-be being blessed by one or more monks. However, I have been given a typewritten document in Thai (kindly supplied by the Bangkok Bank) which fills in some of the gaps in my knowledge of this ceremony. But the Thai lady who gave it to me admits that the whole question of whether this should be considered a Brahmin or a Buddhist ceremony is quite involved and difficult even for Thai people themselves to understand.

Before giving you my interpretation of this document, it is worth mentioning that a Thai astrology book has a few remarks about when not to start building a house: Never on Sunday; never on Tuesday; and especially never, never on a Saturday. A house whose construction begins on any of those three days will bring nothing but trouble to its owner, and Saturday is the worst day of all. Mondays, Wednesdays, Thursdays, and Fridays are all O.K.

So now for the document: It says there are various forms of ceremony for bringing blessings to a new house and its owner. A person's house is his most important possession because he lives, rests, and sleeps in it. So people have been interested from the very earliest times in ceremonies for blessing a new house, and in particular with blessing the act of raising up the main post and placing it in its hole in the ground. According to an old superstition, if the state of "auspiciousness" (called *siri mongkhon* in Thai) is obtained right from the very start of construction, the house-dweller will receive the maximum protection from ill-fortune and will live in serenity, happiness, and prosperity in his new house. The "auspicious inauguration" of the ceremony, therefore, begins with the raising of the main post. (The document points out that nowadays with many larger buildings such as offices and so on, construction starts with the sinking of piles; but there is no further mention of this, and I gather it is not part of the ceremony.)

Although, the document repeats, the universal popularity of the post-raising ceremony goes back to ancient times, the full details of its original form have become blurred over the centuries, and what we see today is just a legacy from the past. So it is regarded simply as a very ancient custom or ritual, but nevertheless everyone has a strong belief in its power to bring blessings on the owner-to-be who performs the ceremony.

Now comes the important bit, and I quote what I hope is a fairly accurate translation of the document: "The ceremony of lowering the post (into the hole) is regarded as a custom of the Brahmin faith; it is much believed in as a means of bringing blessings. But people nowadays have added extra features, such as *saiyasat* or occult powers, and Buddhism has come in too, in the belief that these other aspects will bring even greater blessings." In other words, since both the Brahmins and the Buddhist monks want to wish the owner well and bring him good luck, nowadays they often co-ordinate their efforts to make *siri mongkhon* for him.

The Thai word for a pillar or post is *sao*, and the main post of a house is called the *sao ek* or "first post." The *sao ek* is considered the most important part of the house and should be chosen carefully. It should be of good quality, made from the trunk of a straight tree, and free from knots. The tree should be cut down only during the correct "auspicious" month. Nowadays this is difficult because people mostly buy the post rather than chop down the tree themselves, and one cannot choose the correct month as in days gone by.

Next, the hole must be dug. In olden times the blessings were supposed to be increased still further if the person who dug the hole was given a "good" name specially for the occasion, such as *kaeo* (jewel), *thong* (gold), *di* (good), *mi* (has, or plentiful), *suk* (happy), *ngoen* (silver), or *yuen* (long life).

Also popular is the belief that construction should be started in an even-numbered month, or else in the ninth month. (Just like weddings, in fact.) Nine is always a lucky number in Thailand, because the word for "nine" sounds like that for "progress."

Now to quote the document again: "Monks (that is, Buddhist monks) or a Brahmin priest may perform the ceremony," it says. "It is up to the owner." If the owner chooses monks, the document continues, there should be two, three, five, or best of all, nine of them. There is no chanting involved in this ceremony, but if the auspicious time is near the monks' meal time (no monks may eat after midday), merit can be made by giving them food.

The various things needed for the ceremony with monks are now listed. This includes two tables with white tablecloths – a small one to hold a pair of flower-vases, a pair of candlesticks, and a joss-stick holder needed for paying homage to the Buddha, and a large table to hold the food offerings, holy water. sand, and small silver and gold coins. Also necessary are white paste for anointing; a black pencil to write on the post (in ancient Khmer characters, perhaps an indication of where this ceremony came from); gold leaf; a clove of garlic to rub over the post so the gold leaf will stick; and special leaves for sprinkling the holy water.

The document indicates that several posts are usually brought to the site. The next part of the ceremony (following Brahmin tradition, if I have understood the document correctly) is to choose one particular post which will actually be used as the *sao ek*, or main post of the house.

For this purpose a series of small packages is prepared beforehand. One package contains rice paddy, another package cotton, and others betel-nut, silver, gold, and a cowrie-shell, respectively. Young girls at the ceremony, who must be virgins, each choose a package and then each girl goes and stations herself beside one of the posts. The packages held by the girls are now opened. The post next to the girl holding the package containing the cowrie-shell is the one chosen to be used as the *sao ek*.

This "choosing" ceremony must be very interesting to watch; I have never seen it, alas. Then it is time for the builder to have the chosen *sao ek* placed near the hole already dug for it in the ground.

The next part of the ceremony, says the document, follows the pattern used in the Northeast of Thailand. The oracles are consulted. (I suppose to find the auspicious time for raising the *sao ek* and lowering it into its hole, though the document does not specify.) In the Northeast, sugarcane wood and a banana-tree are often tied to the *sao ek*. A cloth is also tied round the post and pieces of gold and silver are tucked inside. (The color of the cloth must be that of the house-owner's birthday, that is, red if he was born on a Sunday, yellow for Monday, pink for Tuesday, green for Wednesday and so on.) (See Chapter 8.)

At the auspicious time the Brahmin priest or Buddhist monk anoints the post with white paste (after which it becomes known officially as the *sao ek*), applies the gold leaf to the part of the post already rubbed with a clove of garlic to make it sticky, and sprinkles holy water on it. He then takes some sand, on which he casts a spell by blowing gently on it. The owner then lights the candles and joss-sticks, makes a wish for good fortune, *wai*'s (salutes with joined palms) the Triple Gems, and also *wai*'s the *thewada*, or spirits associated with the site of the new dwelling. Offerings of food, spread out on one of the two tables, are also made to the *thewada*.

The monk or Brahmin priest then places various objects in the post-hole in the ground: sand, holy water, gold, silver, flowers, candles, and joss-sticks. Some of the sand and holy water are kept back for placing in the hole in which the second post, the *sao tho*, will later be fixed.

A Buddhist monk is usually chosen to perform this ceremony if the house owner is relatively poor. In such a case it is just one monk, not several. Sometimes the monk sprinkles seashore sand all round the site boundary as protection against thieves and fire.

Before the *sao ek* is placed in its hole, the monk may also place nine miniature *sao ek*, each made of a different kind of wood and known as *mongkhon kao*, at the bottom. I am not sure whether this is in addition to the sand, holy water, and so on mentioned above, or whether it is just an alternative variation of the custom. In any case, all these things such as the gold and silver, the candles, and especially the nine little miniature posts, have the same significance and purpose: They are auspicious and so will help to bring yet more blessings on the house.

After the monk has blessed the *sao ek* and the builders are actually raising it into the vertical position for lowering into the hole, a gong is struck two or three times. This is a Brahmin custom to proclaim publicly that a new dwelling is about to be built. So it seems that, even when a Buddhist monk performs the ceremony, vestiges of the earlier Brahmin tradition and rites are still adhered to, as, indeed, happens with several other types of Thai ceremony.

Another ceremony similar to that of raising the *sao ek* is the laying of the foundation stone, which I imagine is mainly confined to offices, hotels, and so on. It starts off with a most important ceremony, that of propitiating or asking forgiveness from the guardian spirit of the land (for disturbing it by building on its land), and requesting its permission to build. It is believed that if there should be any accidental transgression of the rules of the ceremony afterwards it will not matter once the propitiation ceremony has been correctly carried out. This superstition goes back to very ancient times. It is widely believed that this propitiation will result in happiness, prosperity, and freedom from trouble for everyone concerned.

Nine monks – the lucky number again! – are invited to arrive at the auspicious time. (To be more accurate, the owner of the house-to-be arranges to have them picked up and transported from their temple). Merit is made by giving the monks food and requisites (new robes, medicines, and other necessities). There should be either seven or nine kinds of *kap khao* (dishes to be eaten with rice).

"This ceremony (of laying the foundation stone) is performed by Brahmins," the document continues. This shows, I think, that the ceremony is originally Brahmin. The Buddhist monks are invited simply because, as with any other Thai ceremony, it becomes an opportunity to *tham bun,* or make merit.

The list of requirements for the ceremony is given as: the foundation stone, made of marble; the "star," or horoscope, of the new building; the date and time of birth of the person laying the foundation stone; nine bricks; three pieces each of silver, gold, and an alloy of gold, silver, and copper; flowers with popped rice; and various kinds of food. The place where the foundation stone is laid must be auspicious and far removed from inauspicious places, although the document does not go into further detail.

The stone is anointed in a pattern which accords with the horoscope of the building and the *thewada*, or spirits, are then invited to eat the food provided for them. Sand, previously sifted to make it clean and free from dead bodies of all kinds of creatures, flowers, and popped rice are placed where the stone is to be laid. The bricks, gold, silver, and alloy pieces, nine different kinds of gems and the building's horoscope are also assembled there, and holy water is sprinkled over the stone. A Brahmin priest then blows a conch shell, and a small Brahmin drum called a *ban-do* is struck, after which presumably the stone is laid and cemented in place.

The document ends by saying there are various forms of these two ceremonies (main post and foundation stone) and no one is sure of the details, but everyone performs them because the custom is so old. I suppose it has become deeply etched into Thai society. Those who perform either ceremony feel confident that spirits will not trouble them in the future and that they will live contentedly.

Now I will turn to the later ceremony of moving into a new house. In Thai this is called *khuen ban mai*, literally "going up into the new house"; in former times most Thai houses were built on stilts to avoid flooding in the rainy season.

The auspicious time for moving in must first be found. Saturdays are very unlucky, but Sundays are good. Before the auspicious day, all heavy furniture, such as beds, tables, and chairs, are moved in. At the auspicious hour the owner and his family enter the new house carrying their personal Buddha images, some food, and some money. The Buddha images are set up in their new permanent positions – they must always face either east or north. The wife immediately prepares a meal, even though it is perhaps three o'clock in the morning. This formalizes the act of "moving in." The money is brought in order to ensure future prosperity.

A few days later the religious *khuen ban mai* ceremony is held. This is purely Buddhist, and is a blessing of the new home and a house-warming party all in one. Once again, five, seven, or preferably nine monks are invited. Before they arrive, the white thread known as *sai sin* will have been draped completely round the compound to keep out evil spirits and consecrate everything inside it.

The monks take their places on cushions placed round the wall, with the senior monk on the right. Candles are lit and the ball of white thread is passed from one monk to the next, each holding the thread between the palms of the hands in the *wai* position. For perhaps an hour the monks chant. Afterwards the house-owner offers them food (the ceremony must, of course, take place in the morning). Later everyone kneels in turn before the senior monk, who sprinkles holy water on their heads. (This Buddhist ceremony at home is described in greater detail later in this chapter, under the heading "*tham bun* at home.") One final important rite remains. As the monks prepare to leave, the senior monk anoints every door in the house, and especially the front door, with seven or nine spots of white paste. With that, the ceremony is at an end. After the house (or other type of building) has been in use for some time, the owner may choose to put up a miniature spirit house in a corner of the compound, where the *chao thi*, or spirit of the land, may live.

# Cutting the Topknot

One may occasionally see Thai children with "topknots," or little tufts of hair growing in the middle of an otherwise completely shaven head like a monk's, so that it is hard to tell whether the child is a boy or a girl. You may also sometimes see children with twin tufts on both sides of the forehead, or maybe a sort of pigtail affair at the back. These various styles of topknot, or *chuk*, as they are called in Thai, are grown from early infancy. There is a centuries-old belief which still persists today, especially in the provinces, that a young child who is often feverish or chronically sickly, or even accident-prone, can be cured by growing a topknot. (See Chapter 5.)

Rural folk also follow an old custom of letting the baby choose its own style of topknot – single, twin, or pigtail – by making three crude dolls out of clay, each with the different topknot styling. Whichever doll the child makes a grab for, the parents have its head shaved accordingly. An expert barber does the shaving, which may be carried out at any age from one year old to seven or eight. From then on, the child's head is kept regularly shaved once a week except, of course, for the topknot, which is left to grow.

When the child reaches the age of eleven or thirteen (not twelve, which, being an even number, is unlucky), the ceremony of cutting off the topknot, sometimes known as the tonsure ceremony (*phithi koanchuk* in Thai), takes place. In past centuries this Brahmin rite was one of the most important occasions in a person's life. King Mongkut (Rama IV) had his royal tonsure ceremony in his thirteenth year. It was a magnificent affair lasting seven days, and shears of gold were used to cut off the royal topknot. For children with topknots, and for their families, the tonsure ceremony still retains its ancient significance today. While basically a Brahmin rite, it is also often performed by Buddhist monks.

I once saw this ceremony carried out in rather humble circumstances. The family was a poor one; they were laborers employed on a building site near my home, and the ceremony took place in the corrugated iron shack in a corner of the site which served as temporary living quarters. The little girl with the shorn head and topknot was 11 years old. (I knew she was a girl because I had occasionally seen her around in a dress!) Her parents told me that as a baby she had often been ill, so when she was one year old they began having her head shaved and growing the topknot. Sure enough, after that she got well again and had been completely healthy ever since.

When I arrived to watch the ceremony the family had already draped the sacred white thread known as *sai sin* round the shack to keep out evil spirits. One end of the thread lay in a ball on a mat beside the cushions on which the monks were to sit. The shack had been tidied up and decorated, and the little girl's father had tied her topknot into three neat separate strands.

Soon, the monks arrived. At nearly every kind of Buddhist religious ceremony in Thailand there is always an odd number of monks, again because even numbers are unlucky. In this case, the family being so hard up, there were only three monks. The senior monk took a quick look at the ball of sacred white thread and said, "That won't be long enough." So the child's elder sister dashed off to a nearby shop and soon came back with another ball.

The monk then indicated that besides the white candle which the family had provided along with joss-sticks and flowers, a yellow candle would be required, so back the poor girl went to the shop again. No sooner had she reappeared, panting, with a yellow candle than the monk said, "Two yellow candles!" Poor Sis, she certainly got her share of exercise that day!

The senior monk took the second ball of white thread and made a kind of cat's-cradle round his outstretched fingers. He placed this loop of thread over the edge of a bowl of water so that it dangled in the water, which would later become consecrated when melted wax from the white candle dripped into it during the ceremony. The two yellow candles were placed on either side of the Buddha image on the improvised altar and lit. The ceremony began.

For half an hour the monks chanted, holding the sacred white thread, which was also twined round a large pair of scissors. The little girl knelt facing the monks, her small hands held motionless before her face in a reverent *wai*. From time to time the senior monk stirred the holy water with the white candle.

The chanting stopped. The senior monk placed the loop of sacred white thread round the little girl's topknot. He disentangled the scissors from the white thread, dipped them in the holy water, then snip! snip! snip! It was all over. The topknot that the child had worn continuously for ten years was suddenly no longer there. Only a short, frizzy little tuft remained. The loop of thread was enlarged and placed gently round the child's neck, and the simple but moving ceremony was at an end. As with all ceremonies involving monks, the family then made merit by giving the three monks food.

I have not seen the family for a long time because shortly afterwards they moved on to another site elsewhere. But I suppose by now the little girl has a nice feminine head of hair like any other young lady.

There is also a public Brahmin topknot-cutting ceremony, which is held in Bangkok every January for those even poorer.

## After Someone Dies

When someone dies at home from illness or old age, the body is kept at home for a period ranging from less than one day to seven days. Usually it is three days. Sometimes, however, it may be as long as several months, or, in exceptional cases, a year or even more. But if death has occurred outside the home – whether in hospital, in an accident, or from other causes – the body is always taken straight to a temple.

No matter whether the body is at home or at a temple, as soon as possible after death it is washed, rubbed all over with yellow turmeric or white powder, and dressed in the dead person's favorite clothes in the case of a woman, or best suit for a man. Someone of rank, such as a general, is dressed in full uniform. The body is then laid on a special bed with the head pointing towards the west, because the setting sun symbolizes death. The clothed body is further covered with a cloth up to the neck, leaving the head and the right hand exposed, the latter hanging outwards and downwards.

The same evening, four monks come and chant. (In other ceremonies involving monks, as I have already pointed out, there are always an odd number of them – five, seven, or mostly nine – because even numbers are unlucky. Clearly funeral ceremonies are different.) Relatives and friends arrive, the women always dressed in simple, plain, black and the men in dark suits with a black armband, as in the West. Everyone files slowly past the body, pouring perfumed water over the exposed right hand to purify the body and ask forgiveness for past quarrels and wrongs.

After this, the sacred white cord called *sai sin* makes its appearance. It is tied round the dead person's ankles and round the wrists of both hands, which are folded across the chest in the *phanom mue* position with joined palms clasping a flower and joss-sticks. A loop of the cord is also placed round the neck. These three lengths of cord symbolize the worldly ties of responsibility: The bound ankles mean attachment to property, the cord round the wrists represents worry about the deceased's spouse, and the loop round the neck means worry about the children.

A one-baht coin is placed inside the mouth. Some say this is to ensure the spirit never goes in need, but for most people it is a reminder that the dead cannot take their material possessions with them – not even one baht! The only things one takes with one at death are the *bun* (merit) and *bap* (sins) one has accrued during one's lifetime.

The four monks come and chant for seven continuous nights. In Bangkok the chanting is normally from seven to nine in the evening, but in the provinces it sometimes goes on all night. Members of the family also keep an all-night vigil. During these seven days and nights, as I mentioned above, the body may remain at the house or it may be carried to the temple in an elaborately decorated pavilion-like hearse. Both at home and in the temple, relatives and friends again gather every evening to pay homage, sitting in rows of seats facing the casket, which is raised high up on a stand. A large photograph of the dead person is displayed prominently, and the room is decorated with fresh flowers and beautiful, costly wreaths. Each person in turn goes forward and kneels briefly at a small altar, holding a single burning joss-stick to pay respect to the dead.

Sooner or later the body will be cremated. Just how much later is purely a matter of the family's choice. Cremation normally takes place at a temple, although I believe in the Northeast it is not uncommon for the body to be cremated in an open field on the family's land; in the North, if the family is very poor, the body is sometimes even burnt in the street. Cremations never take place on a Friday, because the Thai for Friday, *wan suk*, has the same sound as another word, spelt differently, which means "happiness."

The burning may be done immediately after the seven nights' vigil or the body may be kept in the temple go down for a year or more. Special merit-making ceremonies are then held on the seventh, fiftieth, and one hundredth days after death. These ceremonies may take place at home or at the temple quite irrespective of where the body is. Monks are given special food – dishes which were the deceased's favorites, lest the spirit go hungry, because it is believed that food taken by monks is transmitted through them to the dead person's spirit.

I have been told by a Thai friend that the whole purpose and meaning of cremation is to liberate the spirit from the body so that it may wander wherever it wants to go. This is one of the many firmly held beliefs about death in Thailand which Westerners may find interesting because they help to give some insight and understanding of the culture and customs of this country.

Some kind of fair or other entertainment is often provided during provincial cremation ceremonies. This usually takes the form of classical Mon music played on traditional drums and gongs, and a dramatic performance such as a *li-ke* or *khon*. If the family is Chinese, the ceremony, called *kong tek*, also involves other features, such as burning paper houses and, in the words of a Thai-Chinese friend, "paper anything

– the idea is to give the dead person a good send-off." Many Thai people believe this entertainment is not only for the sake of the many funeral guests, but also keeps the dead person's spirit company and prevents it from feeling lost or lonely.

In days gone by everyone in the *tambon*, or district, would come to the funeral, no matter whether they were invited guests or not; this was an accepted thing, and all were welcome. There was always plenty of food provided, because some people might have traveled long distances to come to the funeral without a chance to eat anything on the way. Nowadays in Bangkok things are different, with elaborate invitation cards sent out, a rather more formal atmosphere, and only cakes and tea or soft drinks provided in the evening.

The only cremation I know enough about to describe in detail is that of an old lady who died some years ago at the ripe old age of ninety-three. The old lady died in the afternoon. There was just enough time to phone relatives and to wash and dress the body before the bathing rites began at 5.30 p.m. Everyone poured water over the old lady's outstretched hand.

Meanwhile a *sapparoe* (undertaker) had been requested from Wat Prayun, the beautiful temple in leafy surroundings just across the Memorial Bridge on the Thonburi side. The undertaker arrived at the house the next morning. He tied and wrapped the body and put it in a plain wooden coffin. This was then placed in an ornate gilt casket waiting in the hearse outside. Accompanied by close relatives and a single monk, the hearse took the casket to the temple.

After three nights' vigil at Wat Prayun, the family arranged to move the old lady to the country temple at Samrong just outside Bangkok – Wat Suan Som, the Orange Grove Temple, where she had been born. A single monk again accompanied the hearse on its twenty mile journey. At the Orange

Grove Temple the remaining four nights' vigil was kept, followed by the traditional seventh day merit-making practice of giving food to the monks.

The coffin was then removed from the casket and stored together with many others in the temple go down by the edge of a canal. There it remained for eight months until the date chosen for cremation. The old lady's name, Sangwan, was scrawled on the outside of the coffin in red lime for later identification. (This custom explains the superstition which makes the Thai unwilling to sign their names in red; they are afraid they may be signing their own death warrant!)

The two-day cremation ceremony began on a January morning with the arrival at the temple of more than fifty relatives and friends who set about preparing huge quantities of food, enough for all the monks and temple attendants as well as the two hundred or more guests, for two whole days. This was, after all, a country funeral in the old style, not the more formal modern city version.

That afternoon the temple undertaker took the old lady's coffin out of the godown. Expertly and deftly he opened it and took out the remains, by now mainly bones with just a few shreds of flesh, and washed them with water from the nearby canal, which he poured over them from a bowl, letting the water run onto the ground. He then wrapped the remains in a cloth and placed the bundle inside a funeral casket similar to the one in which the body had lain during the seven day vigil eight months before.

A *sai sin*, the sacred cord of white cotton yarn, was tied round the casket. A monk held the end of the cord, symbolically "pulling" the casket, which was actually carried on the shoulders of four sturdy men the short distance from the godown to the temple. There, the casket was placed high up on a stand inside the big *sala*, or hall, with many small gilt tables bearing candles and flowers in front and a large painted cloth forming a mural behind. The old lady's photograph was displayed prominently on a stand. Nearby on a large, low table were gifts to be presented to the monks the following day.

The first evening at the Orange Grove Temple began with solemn music played on classical Mon drums and gongs. This went on from seven p.m. until midnight. At the same time a *khon*, or masked drama depicting stories from the *Ramakian,* the traditional Thai epic drama, was staged in the temple grounds outside. This was a free show put on for the guests and members of the public as a tribute dedicated by the family to the old lady's memory. The show went on until five o'clock the next morning. (In the poorest families, a rather more modest show called a *li-ke* is usually performed. In the cremation ceremonies of better-off families in Bangkok, this tribute to the dead may take the form of a free outdoor film show.)

The next morning, the monks were given food, after which they chanted blessings. Gifts were then presented to them, and in the early afternoon a sermon was delivered by three senior monks, each seated high on a carved gilt chair supported on a low table. After the sermon, a long *sai sin* was passed round so that everyone could grasp it. In this case the *sai sin*, so universal in all Buddhist ceremonies, was a means of communicating blessings from the monks.

Next, a procession formed, led by senior members of the family bearing the old lady's photograph. Three times round the "official" crematorium (not the actual one) the casket was carried to the accompaniment of more solemn music. The Orange Grove Temple, being a modest country temple, has no modern furnace-fired crematorium, and the "official" one was a tall square open-sided pavilion. Its corner pillars were decorated with carved banana-tree stems – a relic from earlier times when country temples did not even have a pavilion like that. In those days, as it was not considered proper or respectful to the dead to place the coffin directly on the flames of the funeral pyre, it was put on a decorated banana-wood platform from the corners of which rose four pillars of the same wood freshly carved into patterns on the morning of the cremation day. These pillars formed a rough open pavilion, and the Orange Grove's "official" crematorium is a more permanent bricks-and-mortar version of the same idea.

After the procession, the casket was placed in position in the "official" crematorium. Then came another age-old ceremony: The symbolic giving of monks' cloth to the body in the casket. Each member of the family in turn placed a folded length of orange cloth on a two-tiered pedestal near the casket, and each piece of cloth was in turn taken away by a monk. This is a reminder of ancient times when poor monks would remove the cloth wrapped round the bones of corpses before cremation to stitch together for use as "rag-robes." Like so many Thai customs of ancient origin, this has now become ritualized as a separate, little ceremony. One of the monks who took a length of cloth at the old lady's funeral was a novice, a young relative who had joined the monkhood just for the two-day ceremony, another fairly common custom.

It was just after this that I arrived at the ceremony. The first thing that struck me was the complete absence of the brilliant colors so evident at most other Thai ceremonies. The scene was a quiet symphony in four colors: The orange of the monks' robes, the massed black ranks of the women's dresses, the men's white shirts, and the deep green of the jungle.

All of us were given *dok mai chan* – small decorative "paper flowers" actually made from wood shavings. We filed slowly past the casket for the *phao lok*, or mock cremation, placing our wood-shaving flowers underneath the casket and giving a *wai*. This again symbolizes the act of setting fire to the casket.

As each guest descended the steps from the "official" crematorium he or she was given a souvenir book. This, too, is a universal custom at Thai cremations. The book is usually about some subject which was a favorite of the dead person. Some memorial books deal with cookery, or flower-arrangement, or gardening; in this case the book was about the old lady's favorite subject, the Buddhist scriptures.

For the real cremation, rich families usually burn the entire ornate casket and its contents. Though large, this old lady's family was not so well-off; the casket had been hired from the temple, so of course it was not burned. The undertaker removed the cloth bundle containing the remains of the body from the casket. A fresh coconut was split open and its water poured over the bundle as an act of purification; coconut water is considered the purest water there is. The bundle was placed in a wood-fired stove in the grounds nearby, and another very short *khon* drama called *khon na fai* ("*khon* in front of the fire") was performed as a final act of respect.

Three rockets were fired into the air to announce the burning. The stove was lit, and the flames consumed the earthly remains of that rather wonderful and very devout old lady who had had six daughters and twenty-six grandchildren. One of those grandchildren is my wife. She says you should never weep when a loved one dies. If you do, the spirit will have to swim through your tears.

# "Placing the Bones"

If one crosses over Bangkok's Memorial Bridge to the Thonburi side, one will see a mass of trees and greenery to the right of the road. Among all this foliage, in a lush setting, lies the temple of Wat Prayun.

Perhaps the most interesting feature of this beautiful temple, built in the reign of King Rama III, is a tall, cliff-like artificial hill in the grounds. Its sides are decorated with all sorts of tiny miniature *chedi*, or pagodas, and with what look like very superior dolls' houses. The hill is about thirty to forty feet high and is surrounded by a moat which is filled with thousands of turtles.

Both the hill itself and the "dolls' houses" have interesting stories behind them. It is said that while reading by candle-light one night, King Rama III noticed that the candle and its melted wax had formed into a mass with a rather attractive shape. He showed this to one of his court noblemen, and the latter ordered a hill to be built at Wat Prayun in the exact shape of the mass of wax.

As for the "dolls' houses," or the miniature *chedi*, these are in fact mausoleums or vaults in which the relics of the dead – the bones and ashes – are kept after cremation. Each "doll's house," or *chedi*, is the property of a single rich family, having been purchased originally for a high price. The bones of generation after generation of the same family are stored in each of these beautifully crafted little places.

I learnt about this some years ago from a Thai friend who invited me to attend a ceremony at Wat Prayun. The head of his wife's family had died several years previously and, after the usual cremation, the bones and ashes had been taken home. They were kept in the house, together with the relics of two grandparents and a great-aunt, for nearly ten years. Then one day some members of the family were chatting with a monk at a provincial temple, and the conversation turned to the relics kept at the family's home. The monk told them that the relics of the heads of families should never be kept at home; they should be taken to a temple and, after the correct ceremony, they should be placed in vaults there.

This ceremony, the Thai name for which is "placing the bones," was the one I attended at Wat Prayun. It began in the same way as many Buddhist ceremonies, with nine monks seated on a raised platform chanting blessings. The relics, a few tiny cloth bags containing the bones, and a slender brass urn holding the ashes, lay on two trays nearby, together with a rectangular plaque inscribed in gilt lettering with the names of the deceased.

When the chanting was over, the family gave the monks food. Then a long strip of white cloth edged with gold was unrolled in front of the monks, to enable the womenfolk to make donations. As any form of contact between a monk or his robe and a woman or part of her dress is forbidden, the women placed their offerings on the white cloth.

After the cloth had been rolled up again, five monks left the platform and the remaining four performed a short special merit-making ceremony for the deceased. Holy water was sprinkled over the relics and over everyone present, using blades of *ya kha*, or elephant grass.

Then the two eldest sons bore the relics and plaque out of the chapel, accompanied by one monk and followed by about sixty relatives and friends, to a narrow passage between King Rama III's artificial hill and the outside wall of the temple. On the side of this wall were a row of plaques identical in size to the one now carried on a tray by one of the sons. A numbered vacant vault-space had already been reserved in the wall, purchased for one thousand baht. Into this vault the monk now inserted the relics.

Then everyone squeezed past in turn, *wai*-ing to the relics with a single burning joss-stick, after which each joss-stick was placed in a jar of sand on the ledge in front of the vault. Tiny vases of orchids and other flowers were also laid here. Finally some coins were placed inside the vault, and a mason cemented the plaque in place, sealing the vault for ever.

## *Tham Bun* at Home

Holding a *tham bun* ceremony (making merit by offering food to monks) in one's own home is something with which every Thai Buddhist is familiar. But it may be a bit of a mystery for Westerners. I have already mentioned that the number of monks invited is usually nine, which is supposed to be lucky; the Thai word for nine, *kao*, sounds similar to the word for "progress."

The ceremony needs careful planning about a month ahead. The householder must visit the temple of his choice to make sure the monks and the abbot will be free to come on the chosen day – which for the average breadwinner must usually be a Saturday or Sunday. Each monk must have a cushion to lean against while chanting, and a mat to sit on. If the temple can supply these, the householder must pick them up the day before the ceremony and return them afterwards. Failing that, some Thai families have their own set of nine monks' cushions and mats which can be borrowed by friends.

The wife must plan all the food for the monks, which must of course be of the highest quality, varied, and abundant in quantity. Several different dishes will have to be cooked early in the day, and dessert and mountains of fresh fruit must be provided, as well as soft drinks, cigarettes, and a set of flowers, candle, and joss-sticks for each monk. They are also given envelopes with money for their day-to-day needs – anything from, say, twenty baht upwards, according to one's means. (In the old days, betel and areca nut were also offered, but no longer, I believe.) Cooking all this food and doing all the arrangements is too much for one person, and the wife calls on female friends and relations to help.

The day before the ceremony, all the furniture is moved out of the living room and the cushions and mats are arranged neatly along the walls and floor. The household's main Buddha image is set up on an altar by the door, immediately to the right of where the abbot will sit. Large yellow candles in holders are placed on either side of the image along with flowers. A bowl filled with water to be consecrated during the ceremony is placed on the floor so as to be within the abbot's reach. (The bowl may be of glass, crystal, or metal, with the exception of gold or silver as it is not appropriate for monks to touch silver or gold. Sometimes a monk's alms-bowl is used.)

The sacred white cord called *sai sin* keeps out evil spirits and protects everyone and everything inside it, so it must be draped round the entire outer wall of the compound or garden. This is usually done by agile teenagers who may have to pass the cord over branches of trees or across tall bushes as they unreel it from its large spool.

The *sai sin* is passed into the room where the ceremony will be held, draped across the Buddha image's right hand, and then passed out again and on round the garden until the premises are completely encircled. Then it is brought back into the room again, to the Buddha image, and from there the spool is placed on the abbot's mat.

The householder must pick up the monks on the day, at about ten a.m. He may hire a minibus or a couple of small pick-up trucks to do this. All the family and their guests must be seated in the room by the time the monks arrive at the house.

The monks take their places, and the ceremony begins with the householder prostrating himself before the abbot and then lighting the two large candles on the altar. He then lights three joss-sticks. (I have held this ceremony twice in my home: Once, many years ago, on my fifth-cycle [sixtieth] birthday, and the second time more recently. On both occasions, I failed to light the joss-sticks properly; the first time I only lit two instead of three, and had to start all over again, while on the second occasion I lit the wrong ends!)

The abbot passes the reel of *sai sin* cord to the monk sitting next to him, and from there it passes from hand to hand until all the monks are holding the white thread. The abbot then lights a white candle and fixes it firmly across the rim of the bowl. As the melted wax drips into the bowl during the chanting, the water inside becomes consecrated. This holy water is called *nam mon*.

The Pali chanting begins with the abbot reciting a few short passages which the householder must repeat after him. Then all nine monks take up the chanting, which continues, deep and sonorous, for thirty to forty minutes, while the family and guests sit with palms joined in a *wai*.

By now it is time to offer the food which has been so carefully and lovingly prepared. The monks' meal must start not later than eleven a.m. to allow them enough time to eat in comfort and be finished before mid-day, after which all Buddhist monks are forbidden to eat. Everyone lends a hand in serving the monks.

When the monks have eaten their fill and relaxed, the dishes are cleared away and there follows a final five-minute period of chanting. During this, the householder pours clean water over his own outstretched forefinger into a small collecting vessel, wishing that the benefit of the food given to the monks may pass on to the spirits of the dead. This water-pouring is cabled *kruat nam*.

Finally, the abbot blesses everyone, including the house itself, by splashing holy water from the bowl. After the monks have left, the householder quietly pours the water from the small vessel onto the ground at the root of a large tree, making another wish as he does so. The *sai sin* draped round the garden is left for the wind to blow away during the next month or so.

## Wai Khru – Paying Respect to Teachers

Not all of Thailand's ceremonies and customs are unique to this country. One such custom found elsewhere in the world is *wai khru* – paying respect to teachers.

This ceremony is held each year in every school, university, and other educational establishment throughout the kingdom. It usually takes place in June or July, soon after the start of the new academic year. The date varies from school to school, but there is one feature of *wai khru* that never varies: it is always held on a Thursday.

As with so many other Thai customs, the reason why it is held on a Thursday is deeply rooted in the past. Thursday's star is the planet Jupiter (the name for "Thursday" and "Jupiter" is the same in Thai – *pharuehat*; the names for Thursday are also similar in sound to "Jupiter" or "Jove" in all the

Latin languages: "Jeudi" In French, "giovedi" in Italian, "Jueves" in Spanish, and so on). Thai astrologers have long held that Jupiter is the "teacher-star" because this planet confers knowledge, concentration, and wisdom. Hence the universal acceptance in this country of Thursday as the day for paying respect to teachers.

On this special day school pupils and university and college students pay respect to their teachers in order to gain merit and good fortune which will help them in their studies throughout the coming academic year. A typical *wai khru* ceremony in a large secondary school starts with the school principal lighting candles and joss-sticks and paying homage to the Buddha image. A senior pupil then reads a prayer or wish aloud. This is repeated in unison by all the other pupils, after which they take a vow to be loyal to their nation, religion, and King, to be good pupils, to behave themselves, and to obey the school rules.

Next, the head pupil of each class in turn presents gifts and flowers to the teachers. There is a school competition for these flower decorations, which pupils have previously spent a lot of time and care in preparing; prizes are awarded by the principal for the most beautiful or original flower arrangements.

The ceremony ends with the school principal delivering a speech and blessing a symbolic book, usually some especially valuable textbook, again symbolizing knowledge. The blessing is done by marking the book with a pyramid of white dots, just as monks do when blessing a new building or company's offices.

The *wai khru* ceremony dates back to the time when Thailand's only centres of learning were the temples. In those days parents took their children to the temple school every year on Thursday with a small golden bowl containing flowers. The children gave these to their teachers, making the same promises as they do today.

Two kinds of flowers were usually included in the bowl. They bore special meanings, as they do to this day. The *khem* flower (genus *Ixora*) has the same name as the Thai word for a needle; so it means the pupils will be sharp-witted and brainy – as sharp as the proverbial needle. The *makhuea*, or eggplant flower, symbolizes respect, and for a very charming and typically Thai reason: Those of its flowers which will later bear fruit always hang downwards. By analogy, students who mentally bow down to their teachers will later receive the fruits of knowledge.

Another kind of plant traditionally presented to the teachers is Bermuda grass, or in Thai, *ya phraek*. The symbolism associated with this grass is interpreted in two ways. No matter how heavily you sit on it, stand on it, or trample it, this kind of grass will never prick you or "retaliate." It is therefore considered very "humble," and students should show a similar humility towards their teachers. Perhaps the second version is more widely accepted: This grass spreads very rapidly across bare ground, so it symbolizes the growth and spread of knowledge in a student.

Besides these and other kinds of flowers, pupils and students also present candles and joss-sticks. The flowers, candles, and joss-sticks together represent the Triple Gem, or *rattanatrai* (also known as *trairat*), that is, the Buddha, his Teaching, and the *Sangha*, or total body of monks – the three concepts at the heart of the Buddhist religion.

Other gifts presented to the teachers include popcorn and paddy (unmilled rice) which have been roasted over a fire in a wire-mesh container like a sieve. During roasting, the sieve is shaken but none of the grains escape. The meaning behind this custom is that the students make a resolve not to stray from good conduct and discipline. Also, just as the corn and rice grains have absorbed heat from the fire, so the students will absorb knowledge.

The ceremony of paying respect to the teachers, so full of all these various symbolic meanings, is one that pupils and students never forget. In later life, whenever they think back to their schooldays, one thing they always remember is this all-important ceremony of *wai khru*.

## *Buat Nak* – Entering the Monkhood

Every male Thai Buddhist aged twenty or older is expected to ordain as a monk at some time during his life, for a shorter or longer period; the length of time is entirely up to him and his family. A favorite time for ordaining is for the duration of the three month *Phansa*, or Buddhist Lent. But many men remain in the monkshood for years – perhaps for their whole life.

The Thai word for "ordination" is *buat,* and the ordination ceremony is known as *buat nak* or *buat phra. Nak* is the Thai form of the Indian *naga*, a huge mythical serpent. According to legend, a *naga* who was a profound admirer of the Lord Buddha and his Teachings disguised himself as a young male human and ordained as a monk. But one night the magic wore off, and he reverted to his natural serpent form, to the horror of his fellow monks. The Buddha is said to have summoned the *naga* and sternly told him that only humans were allowed in the monkhood. "In that case, Lord," said the serpent sadly, "please use my name so that henceforth all young men who are about to be ordained will be called '*naga*'." The Buddha consented, and the custom of using the *naga*'s or *nak*'s name has persisted until today.

(This legend probably also explains why one of the questions asked in Pali during the ordination ceremony is "Are you a human?" The monk-to-be, who has just answered a string of "no's" in Pali, must be on his guard to answer "yes" to this question!)

The first time I attended a *Buat Nak* ceremony was at Bangkok's Wat Yannawa, a temple near the central fish market by the river. I was lucky, because everything took place within the temple compound, all on the same day. (Usually the first part, the head-shaving and *tham khwan*, are performed the night before at the young man's home.)

Watching the head-shaving ceremony may prove a rather traumatic experience for some Westerners because the monk-to-be has his appearance completely transformed in the space of a couple of minutes or so. First his mother, then his father, then some other elderly relative each cut off a single symbolic lock of the young man's hair. Then the professional, a monk if the ceremony is performed at a temple, or a barber if it is at home, gets to work with practiced skill. Using a deadly sharp cut-throat razor, he shaves all of the boy's hair off – even his eyebrows – leaving a clean, shiny scalp. You would hardly recognize him as the same person!

Now the main part of the pre-ordination ceremony begins. This part is called *tham khwan*, and means something like "succoring or soothing the spirit." This is a Brahmin ceremony in which the shaven-headed young man is clad in white robes for purity. There is, however, no fixed rule about this. The *nak* may wear a blue sarong and also a gold or silver gown. But when he finally dons the monk's orange robes he may be said to abandon all worldly things. He kneels near the centre-piece of the ceremony, the *bai si*. This looks something like a slender Christmas tree, and consists of tiers of circular trays mounted cake-stand fashion on a central vertical pole. Each tray bears decoratively folded banana leaves containing cooked rice, and the whole thing is topped with a hard-boiled egg. Kneeling near the *nak* are his parents and one or two close friends. Other relatives and friends cluster around. A lay-preacher well-versed in *tham khwan* carries out this ceremony. He reads out a special sermon via a microphone, addressed to the *nak*. The gist of it is that the monk-to-be owes everything – his well-being, education, life itself, and above all the opportunity to become a monk – to his parents who have raised him and nurtured him since babyhood. Now is his chance to repay that tremendous debt by renouncing all worldly pleasures for a while, so bringing his parents the opportunity to earn merit. The sermon is punctuated from time to time by a crescendo of rhythmic wailing and the crash of a gong. The words are so moving that the *nak* may shake with uncontrollable sobs. He is patted and comforted by his mother and his closest friend.

After the sermon is over, the sacred white thread called *sat sin* is passed round, forming a circle held by the kneeling relatives to protect all inside it from harm. Three candle-holders, each containing three candles, are passed from hand to hand, each person wafting the smoke toward the *bai si*. This procedure is called *wian thian*, literally "circulating the candle," and the candles are also circulated three times. The number three represents the Buddha, the *Dhamma* or Teaching, and the *Sangha* or Buddhist clergy.

Finally everyone starts forming up for the last stage of the outdoor ceremony: The procession. Three times round the outside of the chapel the brilliantly colored crowd marches to the steady one-two, one-two clapping rhythm of a band composed of drums, gongs, and cymbals. Professional dancers bring up the rear. The monk-to-be walks slowly and solemnly under a huge ornate crimson umbrella, hands clasped reverently in salutation round three lotus flowers, joss-sticks, and a candle. Mother, father, aunts and uncles, and a bevy of young girls bear various gifts, including the monk's robes, alms-bowl and other articles to be used by the *nak* after ordination.

Some *nak* ride in this procession on a friend's shoulders – a reminder of earlier days when the *nak* was paraded round the town on horseback, elephant back, or in a palanquin as a public announcement of his coming monkhood. But nowadays walking is usually preferred.

After circling the chapel for the third time, a moment's quiet to *wai* in front of the ornately shaped chapel boundary stone, then the Brahmin ceremony suddenly ends and the Buddhist part just as suddenly takes over as the young man enters the chapel. As he passes inside, he flings coins out after him. I believe this is to symbolize the fact that monks are not allowed to handle money. These coins are eagerly pounced on by friends, because they are supposed to bring good luck.

Once inside the chapel, the formal Buddhist ordination ceremony begins. This consists mainly of chanting in Pali by the monk-to-be and his preceptor and teacher.

## *Phansa* – The Buddhist Lent

"The King orders all the royal temples decorated for Lent every year. He makes offerings to the monks such as sleeping-mats, medicines, Lent candles, oil for their lamps, and joss-sticks. He then pays homage to the Buddha relics and images in all the royal temples within and outside the city." So says the book of *Nang Nopphamat*, which dates from Thailand's Sukhothai Period in the thirteenth century A.D.

But *Phansa*, the Buddhist Lent, goes back much further than that, to the time of the Lord Buddha himself.

One version of the origin of *Phansa* tells how at the start of the rainy season in India (which more or less coincides with that in Thailand), the time of year when farmers have been busy ploughing and planting since time immemorial, a farmer once complained to the Lord Buddha, "Your wandering monks are trampling all over my crops and ruining them." A variation of this story is that the people criticized the monks because while traveling on foot during the rainy season, they caused suffering to small living creatures such as insects and field crabs, which are flooded out of their underground homes at this time of year. The Lord Buddha, hearing these complaints, is said to have made it a rule that all his monks must remain within their own *wihan* or abode during the rains, and temporarily stop their usual custom of traveling far and wide.

This rule still applies. After the beginning of Lent, *Wan Khao Phansa*, all monks must remain "in residence," which means they must spend every night within their own temple and must not travel, except in urgent cases, such as a monk's father or mother being seriously ill. In such cases a special period of seven days away from the temple is permitted.

An invitation card I saw a few years ago, when translated into English, read: "The students' committee of Phra Khanong Phitiyalai (High School) respectfully invite the Director of the School to attend the ceremony of offering the Lent candle on the occasion of *Asalha Bucha* Day and *Khao Phansa* Day, at Wat Bunrotthammaram on July 30, 2520 at 8.00 a.m." The two days mentioned are in fact separate Buddhist occasions. *Asalha Bucha* Day celebrates the day when the Buddha preached his First Sermon after his Enlightenment to five monks in the deer-park at Varanasi

(Banares) in India. It always falls on the full-moon day of the eighth lunar month. *Wan Khao Phansa*, which translated from the Thai means literally "the day of entering Lent," always falls on the following day – the first day of the waning moon in the same eighth month. Both days occur roughly in the middle of July.

Just before *Khao Phansa*, a great many men all over Thailand, especially young unmarried ones, enter the monkhood and most temples throughout the country are crowded with ordination ceremonies. During Lent, which lasts for three months until October, no monks leave the monkhood; likewise, no layman may become a monk during this same period.

The total number of monks in Thailand swells by some 25–30 percent during Lent; at some temples the increase may be two or even three-fold. *Phansa* is considered so important in Thailand that all male government officials and members of the Armed Forces are allowed three months' leave of absence on full pay once during their lifetime, in order to spend at least one *Phansa* as a monk.

The great reverence in which *Phansa* has always been held may have stemmed from the fact that in the early days of Buddhism the monsoon period led to the inaccessibility of solitary dwellings such as caves. Thus monks tended to congregate together in larger groups than at other times of the year, and perhaps they also mingled more among layfolk in the villages. Thus, there was more opportunity for talk on *Dhamma*, the Buddha's Teachings, and more chance for the layfolk to learn.

The fact remains that the start of *Phansa* is celebrated in Thailand in many ways – some religious, others more secular. One of the most important ceremonies is the giving of special Lent candles, often over six feet high and as much as ten inches in diameter. Their huge size allows them to remain alight in the temple chapel throughout the three *Phansa* months, instead of having to be lit afresh every day as is done during the rest of the year. The giving of Lent candles is supposed to bring special merit – the candle is said to become a symbolic "gift of light."

Nowadays these huge candles can be bought in shops, but in earlier times they were made at home by hand from beeswax which was melted down and rolled on a flat board. In the Northeast this is still done; villagers start collecting wax about a month before *Khao Phansa*. When they have collected enough, they roll the candle inside the temple compound. This is always a happy and festive occasion.

In the Northeast, the night before *Khao Phansa*, the candle is placed in a pavilion in the temple, and a ceremony held. The following morning it is placed on a decorated bullock cart and paraded round the village with music and dancing. Prizes are awarded for the best candles from all the villages in the neighborhood before each candle is ceremonially presented to its respective temple and lit to mark the beginning of Lent.

Every year, *Wan Khao Phansa* sees all kinds of merrymaking at temples in Bangkok and in the provinces, including processions, plays, fancy-dress shows, *ramwong* folk-dancing, acrobatic displays, and fire-jumping.

## Making Temple Donations:

### (1) The *Thot Pha-Pa* Ceremony

In Thailand there are many occasions, both public and private, for making donations to a temple. Ordinary people who want to make merit and who, perhaps, have reason to be grateful to a particular temple, often make financial donations. They do so by giving the money directly to the abbot at the temple, always inside an envelope.

But there are also two universal and highly popular ceremonies for making temple donations. These are known as *thot pha-pa* and *thot kathin*. The *thot pha-pa* ceremony can take place at any time of the year before *Phansa* or Lent; while *thot kathin* ceremonies are mostly held in the month immediately after the end of *Phansa,* in mid-October.

There are certain historical relationships between the two types of ceremony which are worth mentioning. Traditionally the main type of offering at both ceremonies was cloth from which to make new robes; but today *thot pha-pa* has become mainly a means of donating money by fundraising, as well as small requisites for monks such as soap, toothpaste, and so on.

Moreover, once a *thot kathin* ceremony has been held at a temple, the monks there have exclusive rights for the whole year to any *pha-pa* cloth left in the fields and forest nearby, as I will describe below. A monk who has found such a piece of *pha-pa* cloth and has sewn it into a robe only to find it is too small for him, is normally allowed to keep it for only ten days; the exception is when this happens after a *kathin* ceremony.

The *thot pha-pa* ceremony can be traced back as far as the time of the Lord Buddha, over twenty-five hundred years ago. *Thot* means "to lay down," *pha* means "cloth," and *pa* is "forest." So the whole name of the ceremony means roughly "to lay down cloth in the forest."

The Lord Buddha told his disciples that they could search in the forest and other empty places for scraps of material from which to sew up robes. (A needle and thread are part of a monk's requisites as prescribed in the Buddhist Doctrine.) The term "rag-robes," meaning robes made from scraps of material found in this way, occurs in several places in the Buddhist scriptures; to this day during the ordination of a monk, the Preceptor recites in Pali: "This Going-Forth has as its support rag-robes."

In the early days of Buddhism in Thailand some twenty-two hundred years ago, monks followed the Lord Buddha's exhortation by wandering round the open countryside collecting whatever scraps of cloth they could find and sewing them into robes. Even today, some monks in rural temples firmly refuse to wear any other kind of robe.

Meanwhile, as the centuries went by, traditions slowly changed. People realised that here lay an opportunity to make merit, and they began deliberately leaving scraps of cloth in fields near temples where monks would be likely to find them. From this it was perhaps only a short step to leaving whole lengths of new orange cloth, or even complete sets of made-up robes, in the fields and woods. It was believed that to gain the most merit, such donations should be made surreptitiously.

In modern times the *thot pha-pa* ceremony has evolved still further. It has now become a means of fund-raising to donate money to the temple of one's choice. The temples chosen are always needy ones, and the money is mostly used for construction or repair work – rather as church fêtes are held in the West to raise money for repairing the church roof.

*Thot pha-pa* ceremonies are well-organized affairs, the groundwork being started many months or even a year beforehand. A special association is set up for each ceremony and appeals are printed in the form of leaflets. One popular way of collecting money for *thot pha-pa* ceremonies is by means of "money-trees." These are set up in public or semi-public places such as shops or large offices, and they symbolize the forest in various ways. They consist of a stout tamarind branch festooned with colored paper. Whenever someone makes a contribution, the 10-baht, 20-baht or 100-baht note is stapled to the string draped across the branch. In time the accumulated money looks like leaves on the tree. Sometimes the notes are folded into the shapes of birds or butterflies.

A piece of orange colored cloth made up to look like a gibbon is also fixed on the tree. It suggests the forest, and the cloth from which it is made represents the *pha-pa* – the scraps of cloth originally found by monks in the forest.

Thus the "money-tree" serves not only as a means of attracting donations, but also as a reminder of the forest from which this very ancient ceremony originated.

## (2) *Thot Kathin*

All religious ceremonies in Thailand – which for practical purposes means almost every kind of ceremony, because most kinds involve the presence of one or more Buddhist monks – must take place on auspicious dates (and times). Important religious festivals generally take place on *Wan Phra*, or holy days, of which there are four in every lunar month. New moon and full moon days are always *Wan Phra*.

The full-moon day of the eleventh lunar month, which always falls in October, is an important day for the monkhood; it is *Wan Ok Phansa*, or the end of Buddhist Lent. After that date, monks are once again allowed to spend nights at temples other than their own, as well as to leave the monkhood, while other men may ordain as monks, which they could not do during the three-month Lent period. It also marks the date when *thot kathin* ceremonies making donations to needy temples in order to make merit can begin. These ceremonies take place at temples all over

Thailand during the whole of the following month, until the next full-moon day, that of the twelfth lunar month, which is also another of Thailand's major festivals: *Loi Krathong*. (See Chapter 2.)

Translated, *thot kathin* means more or less "laying offerings before all the monks in a temple." Historically and traditionally the main offering at *kathin* ceremonies has always been, and still is, cloth from which to make new robes. As with so many traditions, there was a very practical reason behind this one: Lent coincides with the rainy season, and the monks' old robes would have become soiled and perhaps tattered by the end of it. In the past, monks had to make their own robes out of the cloth presented by the layfolk, but nowadays ready-made brand-new robes are usually given. Other gifts are presented as well, such as blankets, kitchen utensils, and various other necessities of temple life, as well as money.

There are certain rules and privileges connected with *kathin* ceremonies. A temple may only accept one *kathin* ceremony a year. Once a *kathin* ceremony has taken place, the monks at that temple have exclusive rights to any *thot pha-pa* cloth, that is, "cloth given in the forest" – robes presented by leaving them in nearby fields in order to gain merit – whereas before a *kathin* has taken place, the cloth may be claimed by the first monk who finds it, even if he lives at a different temple. Also, after a *kathin* ceremony, monks from the temple concerned may leave off their shoulder piece, a carefully folded length of cloth known as *pha sangkhati*, which I know from personal experience is rather difficult to keep in place.

Originally there were two kinds of *thot kathin* ceremony: *chula kathin*, a small affair, and *maha kathin*, a big one. I have been told the people at a *chula kathin* ceremony had to spin the thread, weave it, sew it into a robe, and dye it, all in the one day. This marathon performance naturally drew large crowds of onlookers, who in turn contributed a large amount of money to the temple. But it is said that less merit was gained than at a *maha kathin* ceremony, because all the people doing the spinning, weaving, and so on kept getting in one another's way. Tempers were lost – and with them, merit too. I have not heard of any *chula kathin* ceremonies taking place in recent memory, and I believe almost all *kathin* ceremonies today are of the *maha kathin* type.

A typical *kathin* invitation which my wife and I received read: "Please join to dedicate gifts with our *kathin* association, sponsored by the Supreme Patriarch, to raise funds for building the chapel and *kuti*s (monks' cells) at Wat Inthraram, Tambon Chong Sarika, Amphoe Phatthana Nikhom, Lamphun Province, on Sunday, 30th October 2520, which coincides with the first night of the waning moon of the eleventh month . . ." This was followed by a time-table of the various parts of the ceremony.

We did not go to that one, but we both went to a *kathin* some years ago at Wat Khok Sawang, a temple right out in the middle of nowhere in Chaiyaphum Province. We all went down in three buses. All the way the bus was filled with an ear-splitting thumping of drums, gongs and cymbals, and much loud and cheerful singing. A good time was had by all – and a slight headache by some.

When we arrived, all three gaudily decorated buses were parked overnight inside the grassy temple compound. We sat in the open *sala*, or pavilion, also very festive with colored streamers and the brightly wrapped *kathin* gifts on display. We ate the simple evening meal provided by the temple, and then slept under the clear November sky on the upstairs wooden terrace of a farmhouse nearby.

Next morning the ceremony began with a lively, noisy procession three times round the chapel. After this, the standard *kathin* procedure was followed. The three pieces of *kathin* cloth which make up the set of monks' robes, called *pha trai* ("tri" comes from Sanskrit and ultimately from the same root-word for "three" as the "trai-" in "triangle" and "tricycle") were placed before the monks seated in the chapel. The president of the *kathin* association then announced in Pali: "We present these robes to the *Sangha* (assembly of monks). Please perform the *kathin* ceremony." A monk then said: "These persons have brought this *pha trai* with pure intentions. If any among us considers one of his brethren to be especially well versed in the scriptures and teachings of Buddha, please say his name." Another monk then suggested a name – I believe it was that of the abbot. After repeating the question twice more with no dissenting voice, the monks said *sathu* (amen). Two monks then picked up the *pha trai* and chanted: "This temple is deserving of this *pha trai*. The *kathin* ceremony has been performed correctly." After again repeating this twice more without dissent, the abbot retired and put on the new robes. The other *kathin* gifts were presented and the ceremony was over.

At every *kathin* ceremony, after the merit-makers have left, the monk who has by popular vote acquired the new robes repeats solemnly three times before all the other monks, "I shall wear this *pha trai* as my robe." The other monks chant a blessing. The merit associated with the new set of robes is shared by them all.

# CHAPTER FOUR

# Customs

## Some Social "Do's and Don'ts" in Thailand

I have heard it said that no Thai university undergraduate will ever put on a graduate's gown – not even their elder brother's or sister's, "dressing up" for a moment's fun. It is a very natural and understandable superstition that this would bring an undergraduate bad luck, and they would never become a graduate if they did it: a Thai version of "tempting fate," in fact. Every country has its own superstitions, many of them so deeply ingrained that they have become social customs. Here are some Thai customs and manners – things that are or are not "done."

Thais consider the head the most important and honored part of the body; and, conversely, the foot is the most degraded. Touching anyone on the head is a great insult. Even a friendly pat on the head, or tousling someone's hair, is only done between brothers, sisters or the closest friends – and, even then, only if there is not too big a difference in age.

Similarly, pointing at anyone with your foot is extremely rude. In fact, using one's foot for any purpose for which hands are normally used, such as kicking a door shut, is also very bad manners in Thailand. We Westerners are apt to use our feet for un-foot-like actions much more than Thais do, and this has given rise to a very telling Thai expression for the feet: *mue farang* or "*farang* hands"! (*Farang* is the colloquial term for any Westerner.)

"The pattern of social organization in the Siamese hierarchy demanded that, where a difference in social level existed between individuals, it was accompanied by a corresponding spatial separation in height and sometimes distance." So wrote a Western scholar a few years ago about 17th century Siam. "An individual with a superior position on the social scale would at least have his head above that of his inferior," he continued. "Among present-day Thais one still finds many examples of this custom, as when students duck their heads when they pass in front of a seated teacher." Western readers who have attended Thai ceremonies will certainly have had similar experiences themselves when, for instance, a servant has had to pass in front of them.

Thai people in general, in the relaxed atmosphere of their own homes and especially in the provinces where houses tend to be sparsely furnished, usually sit on the floor cross-legged or with their legs tucked beneath them. If a child wants to walk past an adult seated in this way he should crawl past so that his head is lower than that of the adult – or at least attempt to do so by bending down as low as possible while he is passing.

A Thai friend tells me that even in the more sophisticated atmosphere of Bangkok society, seniority is still very important; a younger person should never sit with his head at a higher level than an older one. He says his younger sister's girl friends, though only perhaps two or three years younger than him, would never dream of sitting on a chair if he happened to be sitting on the floor.

The late Phya Anuman Rajadhon, in his monograph *Thai Traditional Salutation*, published by the Fine Arts Department, throws some interesting light on this question of the head. He says the Thai deems his head sacred, probably because it is the seat of an individual's *khwan* or vital spirit, which confers strength and health. The *khwan* is very sensitive, and if subjected to indecorous behavior it will feel injured and leave its abode in the body to stray somewhere in a forest. While the *khwan* is absent, its owner will suffer a weakening of his "dignified splendor," followed by bad luck and ill-health. With such an idea handed down from generation to generation over a very long period of time, the sacredness of the head is deeply embedded in everyone's mind. If the hand that touches another's head is that of a woman, the man will instantly lose his "dignified splendor," for a woman's hand is acutely adverse to the *khwan*.

This explains why Thai people, especially men, refuse to walk beneath a clothesline on which female clothing is hanging, especially lower garments such as sarongs or skirts, for fear their head will be touched by them. So when women's clothes are hung out to dry, a very low clothesline is used, and everyone walks round it instead of under it.

And while we are on the subject of walking round something or somebody, if anyone at all – even a young child – is lying on the floor resting or asleep, no Thai will ever step over such a prostrate person, no matter how much of a hurry he is in. Again, it simply "is not done." One must always walk round – never step across.

# *Khun*: An Everyday, But Deep, Word

In Thailand, as I have mentioned, the greatest importance is attached to seniority, and to the height of the head. The head of a junior person should never be higher than that of a senior in age or rank. The Thai friend I referred to earlier told me his young sister's girl friends have all come to know him in the first place through his being the elder brother of their friend. So they invariably address him as *phi*, a word meaning "elder brother or sister," and they take care not to sit at a higher level than him. But many of his colleagues in the office where he works are no older than his sister's friends, yet none of them would ever dream of calling him *phi*. The office is a more westernized institution, I suppose, in which everyone is equal. (Yet I've heard some of the girls in our office call other girls *phi*. Maybe they're old schoolmates, and the one addressed as *phi* was in a higher class.)

The opposite of *phi*, by the way, is *nong*, "younger brother or sister." I'll deal with these and other words for family relationships in Chapter 7.

Now I shall deal with an important word which I feel certain even very recent arrivals in Thailand will have heard: *khun*. What does it mean?

Well, the form in which we usually meet it is before a first name, when it carries the meaning of "Mr.," "Mrs.," or "Miss," as the case may be. It also means "you." But if we look it up in the Thai-English dictionary, we find the following rather surprising meanings: "*Khun*, noun, prefix: merit, advantage, virtue, good, goodness, services, help, good offices . . . A personal pronoun in the second person equivalent to 'you,' formerly employed as a mark of respect, but nowadays universally used by men and women in addressing equals of both sexes . . . " "Formerly employed as a mark of respect"; those words are important if we as foreigners are to understand the favorable undertones associated today in the minds of Thai people with *khun*, and so are the meanings of "merit, virtue" and so on.

In conversation, Thais mostly avoid the use of the second-person pronoun ("you") and instead use the name of the person they are addressing, especially if that person is only a casual acquaintance. Instead of asking "Do you play golf?" a Thai will ask "Does *Khun* Aroon play golf?" Servants also tend to use their own names instead of "I." Westerners will no doubt have heard their servants, especially if their English is not very good, say "Madame, please excuse Malee (if that is her name). Malee cannot find good chicken in market today."

But two Thais who don't know each other's names will address each other as *khun*, meaning "you" exactly as is done in the West. If a Thai wants to attract a stranger's attention (for instance, if a car driver wants to ask a passing pedestrian the way), he'll shout *"Khun! Khun!"* Translated directly into English, this comes out as "You! You!" In the West this sounds rude – it carries overtones of "Hey, you!" But in Thai, because of the good associations of the word *khun*, it is entirely polite. There is no trace of rudeness whatever: No offence meant and none taken. On the contrary, *khun* is rather complimentary.

It's even more polite to shout *"Khun khrap!"* or *"Khun kha!"* depending on the sex of the person who is shouting: *khrap* if it is a man, *kha* for a woman. This is roughly the equivalent of shouting in English "You, sir!" or "You, madam!" In the English case, of course, which phrase is used depends on the sex of the person being shouted at rather than on the person doing the shouting.

The words *khrap* and *kha*, when used on their own, also

mean "yes" (that is, they express agreement). As just mentioned, *khrap* is spoken only by a male, and *kha* only by a female. These words also give an added politeness when used at the end of a sentence, and they are used with great frequency in this way when talking to an equal or a superior. Many Westerners conversing with Thai friends in English have probably had experiences along the following lines. Foreigner: "You're not coming tomorrow, then?" Thai Friend: "Yes." The Thai means "No, I'm not coming," but what he or she is really doing is to mentally translate the Thai *khrap* or *kha* to mean "Yes, you are right!"

Another interesting difference between Thai and Western customs is found in the traditional postcard message sent by holidaymakers to their less fortunate friends or relatives back home. "Wish you were here!" writes the Westerner. "Wish you were THERE!" writes the Thai. He is putting himself in the place of the postcard's recipient – a very thoughtful way of expressing the message.

## Some Other Social Norms

Here are a few more customs which are considered more or less social norms in Thailand. Some of them are strictly adhered to as a matter of essential etiquette; others are less so, and being to some extent rooted in superstition, are observed for one's own good rather than other people's. But by and large, there is a reason behind all these norms.

In the section called "After Someone Dies" in Chapter 3, I have already mentioned the fact that many Thais refuse to sign their names in red ink or with a red pencil because it is considered unlucky to do so; but it is worth repeating here. I wonder if all those who follow this rule realise its origin.

The reason is that the wooden coffins containing the bodies of the dead, which are stored in temple go downs while awaiting cremation, have the deceased's name scrawled at the side of the coffin – in *red* lime. So if you sign your name in red, it's like signing your own death warrant! A very simple and logical superstition.

No Western man would ever dream of entering a church without first removing his hat. Just as surely, no Thai of either sex will ever enter a temple, or any private house, without first removing his or her shoes. Nowadays this is mainly an act of politeness, but the origin of this custom dates back to the distant past when all roads were dirty, and in the rainy season very muddy, too. No one wants dirt brought into the house (remember how mother used to bawl at us when we were children, "Take your filthy boots off – just look at what you've done to my carpet!"); so everyone takes off their shoes. (I had learnt about this sensible Thai custom from a "Hints for Visitors" brochure before I first arrived in this country many years ago, and I brought two pairs of slip-on shoes with me. I haven't worn a pair of lace-up shoes since.)

Another social rule in Thailand which doesn't need any explanation is that no one ever wears black to a wedding, or any other kind of party. Those who are in mourning, and are therefore wearing black, must beg permission from their dead relative's or friend's spirit to come out of mourning temporarily, just for the occasion of the wedding or party. Also, one should not wear a certain shade of pale blue-green at a wedding, because the Thai name for this color is *sok*, which also means "sad."

Never sleep with your head facing towards the west, runs another superstition. The setting sun symbolizes death. There is a well-known Thai legend about this. One of the gods, Phikhanet (Ganesha), caused offence to Phra Narai (the Hindu god Vishnu). As a punishment, Narai removed Phikhanet's head, and told him he must find someone sleeping with his head towards the west and take that head to use for his own, or else forever remain headless. Since only the dead sleep with their heads facing west, this was no easy task; but after long searching, Phikhanet found an elephant sleeping in that position. He removed the animal's head and placed it on his own body. The god Phikhanet, with an elephant's head, forms the emblem of Silapakorn University and the Fine Arts Department.

According to another widely accepted superstition, it is unlucky to make someone a present of a sharp or pointed object such as a knife or sword. The recipient of such a present should always make a very small token payment to the giver – say, one per cent of the article's value. In effect this means that the sharp-pointed gift is being "bought" instead of being received as a pure gift. If it is a gift, this means the friendship between giver and recipient is ruined, and enmity will grow between them.

# The *Wai*

Nothing is more typical of Thailand than that charming and universal greeting, the *wai*. The information about this that follows comes partly from the late *Phya* Anuman Rajadhon's slim monograph "Thai Traditional Salutation" in the series on Thai culture published by the Fine Arts Department, and partly from friends and my own experience.

The *wai* is so well known to every Westerner who has ever stepped off an incoming aircraft at Bangkok's Don Muang airport (or, for that matter, who has ever been greeted by a

Thai Air hostess when stepping into a Thai Airways aircraft at any airport around the world) that I feel it is hardly necessary even to describe it. However, I will do so for the sake of those readers who have yet to visit Thailand.

The *wai*, says *Phya* Anuman, is a sign of greeting or mutual recognition made by raising both hands, palms joined, to a position lightly touching the body somewhere between the chest and the forehead.

So much is common observation. But until I had read *Phya* Anuman's instructive booklet, I did not realise that the higher the hands are raised, the greater the respect and courtesy conveyed. Also, the person who is junior in age or social rank is the first one to give the *wai*. The senior person immediately returns the greeting, usually with the hands raised no higher than the chest. (It is very bad luck for an older person to *wai* a younger one first, and is supposed to take seven years off the younger person's life.)

For instance, a group of university students passing their lecturer or professor (*achan* in Thai) in the university grounds will *wai* with almost military precision, hands raised to their faces and heads bent forwards. The person returning the students' *wai* may *wai* with the hands raised to chest level, or if he is preoccupied or in a hurry he may just raise one hand or even merely nod his head to acknowledge the greeting.

In general, a *wai* may be made while sitting, standing, walking, or even from one's sick-bed. If you can remember my description of Thai etiquette regarding the height of the head in relation to that of a senior, you will not be surprised to learn that a junior person who is standing and wants to *wai* to a senior who is sitting, will automatically stoop or bow the head while making the *wai*. This is a matter of ordinary good manners, ingrained in every Thai since infancy.

The raising of the hands in a *wai*, and lowering them after the *wai*, are never done with a sudden or jerky movement, but as slowly and gracefully as possible. The upper arms and elbows are kept close to the body, and the joined hands are bent slightly inwards.

The traditional form of the *wai* can be seen at its most perfect in Thai classical dance and drama performances, and in ceremonies such as the *wai khru*, or students paying respect to their teachers, which I described in the previous chapter. In dance and drama especially, the graceful and subtle hand movements begin with the performer placing his or her hands together, palm to palm, with the fingertips of both hands curved slightly inwards towards each other so as to form the shape of a green lotus bud, or *bua tum*. In formal religious ceremonies, the hands making the *wai* will often clasp an actual green lotus bud and joss-sticks, to be later offered in homage to a monk or Buddha image.

During a Buddhist sermon, or while a chapter of monks is chanting in Pali from the Scriptures, monks and layfolk alike will remain seated or kneeling with their hands in the "lotus-bud *wai*" position throughout the ceremony, which may last for forty-fice minutes or an hour – sometimes even longer. Fatigue is eased by keeping the upper part of the arms tucked against the sides of the body.

Buddhist monks in Thailand never return a *wai* from any layman, however advanced in years or exalted in rank – not even from His Majesty the King. Instead, they acknowledge the *wai* with a nod or a friendly smile, and perhaps a few words of greeting. The exception to the latter is during the daily alms round; after putting food into a monk's bowl, the householder will kneel and *wai*, but the monk must completely ignore this greeting which is an essential part of the act of merit-making.

A question which may occur to foreigners is whether a younger man would *wai* to an older woman in the same way as he does to an older man, and whether the older woman would return the young man's *wai* in the same way as the older man does. The answer is, yes; assuming the younger and older persons are of the same social rank, it is the difference in age that counts, not the difference in sex.

## More Elaborate Forms of the *Wai*

The more elaborate forms of *wai* which I shall now describe represent rather deeper gestures of respect. My main source of information about these forms is again the late *Phya* Anuman Rajadhon's booklet, "Thai Traditional Salutation," published by the Fine Arts Department.

In the type of greeting known as the *krap*, the person paying respect begins by kneeling with the upper part of the body in an upright position, the haunches resting on the heels or the upturned soles of the feet. The hands are held in a "lotus-bud *wai*" just below the chest. They are then raised to the forehead, still in the *wai* position. Next, the hands are placed on the floor, palms downwards, in front of the knees. The right hand is placed on the floor first, followed by the left, the two hands being slightly separated. The body is now bent down until the forehead touches the floor between the two hands. Then the body is raised again to the upright position with the hands held to the forehead in the *wai* position, and the process is repeated twice more – that is, three times in all.

This is the salutation which all monks (and all lay people) perform in front of the Buddha image in a temple, during every kind of ceremony. (I had to do it as part of my ordination ceremony when I became a monk, and again when I disrobed.) The significance of the threefold repetition is that the first salutation is to the memory of the Buddha, the second one to his Teaching, and the third to the *Sangha*, or total body of Buddhist monks everywhere.

Monks also perform the *krap* before meditation if the place where they are meditating contains a Buddha image. This type of *krap* is known as the "five-point prostration" (*benchangkha-pradit* in Thai); the five points are the forehead, the two hands, and two knees.

The *krap* can also be performed as an act of respect towards living people such as one's elders. In this case the hands are not placed flat on the ground but remain in the lotus-bud *wai* position, with the forehead lightly touching them.

In the *mop krap* the person paying homage kneels before the respected person with hands raised to the chest in lotus-bud *wai* and immediately lowers the hands, still in the *wai* position, until they touch the floor, while at the same time bending the body until the forehead rests on the two thumbs.

The word *mop* really means "to sit in a crouching position," and there is also an alternative form of the *mop krap* in which the person crouches sideways, legs tucked backwards and inwards and hands again resting on the floor in lotus-bud *wai*. The hands are then raised, still in a *wai* and with the elbows kept on the floor for support, until the hands reach the forehead which has been bowed downward to meet them.

In earlier times the *krap* was also performed as a rather interesting act of atonement or conciliation to *Mae Thorani Pratu*, literally "Mother Earth of the Doorway," the spirit which was supposed to dwell inside the raised threshold of a door. Anyone inside the Royal Palace who unwittingly stood on such a raised threshold, instead of stepping over it, was believed to have committed a grave wrong, and the Palace guards standing by the doorway would make that person atone by performing a *krap* and offering prayers and joss-sticks. Today, these old-style raised wooden thresholds are still fairly common at the entrances to rural houses, and Thai people universally and automatically step over them, never on them.

## Music – Classical and Western

Some years ago I was entertaining three visitors from England with some Thai folk songs on my record-player. Like all modern Thai popular music, these songs were in the familiar do-re-mi-fa scale which all Westerners have known from early childhood. Two of the songs had a lilting accordion accompaniment. Perhaps it was because my guests were English that I suddenly noticed something which I had missed whenever I had listened to these particular songs before. "What does this music remind you of?" I asked them on the spur of the moment. They looked a bit blank at first, but after a moment or two they admitted it sounded vaguely familiar although they couldn't quite put their finger on it. "Don't you think it sounds rather Scottish?" I asked, and they immediately agreed it did.

One of my three friends happened to be a keen music enthusiast. "Ah," he said, "that's because these Thai songs are written in the pentatonic scale, which is also quite common in Scots music . . . " and he then launched into a long technical explanation which left me and my other two guests quite lost.

But I was curious to know more, so later on I spent a couple of hours in my musical friend's hotel room trying to understand what he meant. Although he had only been in Thailand a short time he had spent many hours at the Fine Arts Department talking to their experts, and he already knew quite a lot about Thai music, both "classical" and "modern." The gist of what he told me was this. (I will try to keep it as simple as I can.) On the ancient Thai classical scale, which is still used today as the accompaniment to classical dancing and drama and for temple music, the intervals between all the notes are exactly the same – in theory, at any rate. In the Western do-re-mi-fa scale (the white notes on the piano) this is not the case; there are two semi-tones – one between the third and fourth notes, and the other between the seventh note and the octave. Broadly speaking, these two semi-tones are what give any melody on the Western scale a feeling of character, and the listener a sense of orientation: The tune sounds as though it ought to end on the keynote, and it usually does.

With the classical Thai scale there is no such sense of orientation for the listener, because the intervals between all notes are the same; the notes are evenly spaced, so that if all of them were used, the melody would sound colorless and dull. This difficulty seems to have been realised centuries ago, and ancient classical Thai melodies overcame it by leaving out two notes in every octave.

It so happens that the two notes that are left out are spaced the same distance apart as the fourth and seventh notes on the Western do-re-mi-fa scale. Leaving out these two notes restored a feeling of character to the old classical melodies and "oriented" the listener. Because such a scale leaves out two notes and so contains only five notes instead of seven, it is known as the "pentatonic" scale. (In the Thai and Western scales alike, the eighth note is exactly an octave above the first; but of course no other notes are quite the same on the two scales.)

The Western scale was introduced into Thailand about 150 years ago, and at some later date country folk songs began being composed on this scale. But perhaps from force of habit, they often kept to the old classical custom of using the pentatonic scale by leaving out the fourth and seventh notes.

Melodies using the pentatonic scale have a special quality of their own which cannot be described in words, but can only be appreciated by listening to them. This is true whether such melodies are on the Thai classical or the Western scale. And since, as my musical friend pointed out, many Scottish folk tunes also use the pentatonic scale, this explains the Great Thai-Scottish Music Mystery.

If you have a piano in your home, and you have not yet stopped reading this because you are far more knowledge-able musically than I am, try experimenting with the pentatonic scale. The easiest way to do this is to use only the black keys; this comes to the same thing as leaving out the fourth and seventh white notes in the scale of C-major (which uses only the white keys). You will find you can play many Scottish tunes on the pentatonic scale; "Auld Lang Syne" and "A Hundred Pipers" are two well-known ex-amples. And if you listen to some of those lovely Thai clas-sical melodies on the radio and can memorize them, you will find you can play them on the black keys too. The "*Loi Krathong*" melody is a good example.

To end with, here are some rather brief details of Thai classical instruments, on which, as I said, all tone-intervals are – or are supposed to be – exactly equal.

The *ranat*, rather like a curved xylophone, is made of graduated hardwood bars. A commonly used type of wood is *mai chingchan*, or *Dalbergia* to botanists. The wood is specially cured in certain provinces. Exact tuning is achieved by sticking lumps of beeswax containing lead filings onto the underside of each bar. I recently borrowed a Thai friend's *ranat* for a month or so, and discovered that each bar had been carefully and individually hollowed out underneath to give it the correct pitch. This *ranat* was quite old – it had belonged to my friend's teacher's teacher! – and during its journey by car to my house a few of the beeswax lumps had dropped off from some of the bars. This was immediately evident when I started playing; the notes with the missing lumps were way off key. I had to stick the lumps on again by melting them.

The other main instruments which provide the melody are the *khong wong yai*, a series of hump-shaped brass discs arranged in a circle inside which the player sits; its smaller cousin the *khong wong lek*; and the *pi nai*, which is something like a flute.

Listening to Thai classical music played on these instruments is a rather strange sensation to Western ears because of the different tone-scale. But all the same, the characteristic "flavor" of the pentatonic scale comes over very strongly.

## Worshipping Brahma and Other Deities

Ordinary Thai people worship a great many deities, sacred objects, guardian spirits, spirits of former living heroes and heroines, and lesser spirits – as readers of this book will have discovered already. All these entities are worshipped primarily in order to ask for the granting of a wish or favor, and to render thanks when the wish has been granted. Each entity has his or her favorite food, entertainment, and type of transport, and these special tastes must be taken into account when homage is being paid.

Although perhaps the worship of these deities should more correctly be described in the next chapter – Beliefs and Superstitions – I am dealing with them here because they are such a basic part of everyday Thai life that they are indeed "customs."

I must make it absolutely clear, however, that the overwhelming majority of Thais are Buddhists, and the Teachings of the Lord Buddha govern their lives. The worship of these various deities is always subsidiary to Buddhism. Yet, in a special Thai way, the people manage to combine both – as readers will have already gathered with regard to Brahmin customs and ceremonies.

Of all the deities so worshipped, Brahma, Lord of the Heavens, is the highest, and the beautiful shrine of Phra Phrom, or Lord Brahma, just inside the grounds of the former government-owned Erawan Hotel, which later became the Grand Hyatt Erawan Hotel, at the corner of Ploenchit and Rajdamri Roads, is a place held in the deepest reverence. (One of my early but indelible memories of Bangkok is of the time when, as a Colombo Plan expert, I had a minibus and driver assigned to me for the duration of my contract. Every time we drove past Rajprasong crossroads, usually at quite a spanking pace, my driver took both hands off the wheel at the same time to *wai* to Phra Phrom. I used to shut my eyes in silent prayer too, for a different reason . . . But I got used to it in time.)

In the centre of the four-sided open shrine sits the handsome golden god. He has four faces and eight hands. One hand holds a book (the Vedas or Hindu scriptures), the second a scepter, the third a drinking vessel, the fourth a string of beads, the fifth a conch shell, the sixth a staff, the seventh a hollow disc, while the eighth lies across his breast.

The shrine, built in 1956, has an interesting history. It was built by the Erawan management almost by chance, owing to a string of misfortunes which occurred during the construction of the hotel itself. One mishap followed another, culminating in the sinking at sea of a ship bringing marble for the hotel. This was too much for the superstitious construction laborers. There must be evil spirits hanging around, they said. They demanded that something be done about it, or they would down tools to a man (and woman).

A Brahmin expert was consulted. He pointed out that since the name "Erawan" already chosen for the hotel was the name of the three-headed elephant which the Lord Brahma rides, the "Erawan" ought not to go riderless: Brahma should be there too. So the shrine for the Lord Brahma was built in the hotel grounds, and from then on, there were no more accidents.

All kinds of people, from the hotel management and staff to the general public, worship at the shrine and make frequent donations and offerings. Passengers in passing buses *wai* to the Lord Brahma. The correct times for worship are from seven to eight a.m. and seven to eight p.m. Asking for a wish to be granted should be done in the evening, when the shrine glitters in the glare of powerful spotlights and classical dancers may sometimes be seen performing for Brahma's entertainment, paid for by someone who has been granted an important favor.

But offerings big or small can be made at any time, in cash or kind. Humbler offerings take the form of flowers, sweet-smelling garlands known as *phuang malai*, gold leaf, and food. All day long people are seen offering these things, kneeling in homage at the four special stools provided, rather like miniature pulpits. Inside a special lamphouse burns a perpetual flame at which joss-sticks and candles can be lit.

Wandering along the pavement in Ploenchit Road near the Rajprasong crossroads you can see several groups of garland makers and vendors busily threading jasmine flowers onto lengths of cord. They also have teak elephants in various sizes for sale. These, too, are offerings to Brahma – remember, his favorite steed is an elephant.

But after an elephant has been consecrated to the Lord Brahma, that is not the end of it. The elephants are resold and the proceeds together with the even larger financial donations to the shrine itself are put to good use for the community. In 1988 the Than Thao Mahaphrom Erawan Hotel Foundation was set up with its offices now inside the present hotel, to manage the funds collected. From the opening of the shrine in 1956 up to the end of 1992, a total of 120 million baht had been collected. This money has been donated to more than three hundred hospitals all over the country to buy modern medical equipment. And it is an ongoing activity, day in, day out. The money never stops coming.

Some years ago the management of the original Erawan Hotel gave me a seven-page document in Thai, which a friend has kindly translated for me. It was entitled "Details concerning the worship of Brahma the Great, Lord of the Heavens."

Objects to be used in general worship, says the document, should consist of seven joss-sticks, one candle, seven flowers of different colors or one *krathong* (a kind of basket similar to those floated on the water on *Loi Krathong* Day) which must be of seven different colors, and one *krathong* of popped rice. The seven joss-sticks must be used on every occasion of worship and may only be omitted if it is absolutely impossible to obtain them, as for instance when you are abroad, in which case you may simply *wai*. The same applies to the other objects.

When worshipping at the shrine, seven pink or white lotus flowers, roses, garlands of jasmine or of other flowers may also be used. Depending on the strength of your devotion, a seven-colored garland, seven or fourteen feet long, is even better.

When asking for a favor at the shrine, a *krathong* of seven different colored flowers must be offered. But if you are asking for a favor from elsewhere (in Thailand, presumably), the last three items may be either omitted or included according to strength of devotion. You should make the following statement:

"I beg to offer worship to the Great Lord Brahma, Lord of the Heavens, with these offerings. May he be happy and out of his great kindness make me happy too, bring me progress and prosperity, make me strong and free from sickness, give me a long life and allow me to find the means to make a living . . . " (make additional wish as required).

Objects for formal worship and offerings must consist of seven *krathong*, each with flowers of seven colors; seven *krathong* of chopped sugar cane and seven of popped rice, each decorated with a rose; seven pure wax candles, each of one baht weight; two coconuts with the green skin left on but with top and bottom sliced off to allow them to stand upright; two bunches of choice *nam thai* bananas; and seven joss sticks. The candles should be fixed on a plate, one in the middle and the rest spaced equally round the edge.

When requesting a favor, if possible, you should go to the Erawan shrine, but if you live a long way away you can do this at home by lighting seven joss-sticks which should then be stuck in a plant-pot out of doors. On no account should they be stuck directly in the ground. An offering of a seven-colored garland fourteen feet long should be promised when requesting the following favors: success, such as a rise in salary; passing an examination; the granting of a child to a barren woman; a trip overseas; repayment of an outstanding debt; protection during a trip abroad; carrying out a dangerous task; taking money upcountry; and prosperity, in business for instance.

Besides Brahma, there are also various highly respected gods, such as Indra and Vishnu; these are known collectively as *thewada, thewa*, or *thep* (as in Krung Thep, the Thai name for Bangkok).

There are also *Luang Pho* or Buddha statues. An hour's ride by car or train due east of Bangkok lies the pleasant provincial town of Chachoengsao. Just outside the town is the temple of Wat Sothon, which houses one of Thailand's most revered Buddha statues, Luang Pho Sothon.

Parents of a sickly child who consult a senior and respected monk at their local temple about a cure for the child, as described in the next chapter, are often advised to beg a special Buddha statue to "adopt" the child and look after it, which will make the child well again. Among the hundreds of specially revered Buddha statues in Thailand, one of the most famous is Luang Pho Sothon at Chachoengsao.

A legend tells of the origin of the Luang Pho Sothon statue. More than a thousand years ago, so the story goes, three brothers suddenly appeared floating down the Bang Pakong River near Chachoengsao. They were not human brothers, but Buddha statues.

No one knew where they had come from. The largest of the three continued floating down the river to the sea, where he followed the upper coastline of the Gulf of Siam, finishing his journey in the Mae Klong River at Samut Songkhram.

There the local people invited him to come ashore and dwell in the temple of Wat Ban Laem, which he did.

The second brother-statue followed a similar course, but floated up the Chao Phya River towards where Bangkok now stands and then along Khlong Bang Phli at Samrong. As he passed the first temple along the canal, Wat Nam Daeng, or Red Thorn Temple, the local folk tried to persuade him to enter the temple by lighting joss-sticks and worshipping him, but to no avail; he did not stop, and they were powerless to make him do so. However, when he reached the next temple, Wat Bang Phli Yai, the people there first paid homage to him and then used a sacred white *sai sin* cord to try to pull him ashore. This time they were successful. Luang Pho To, as he is known, is much worshipped.

The third brother came to rest on the bank of the Bang Pakong River at the spot where Wat Sothorn now stands. Again the local people tried to persuade him to come ashore, and again they were unsuccessful until they paid homage and tied a *sai sin* round him. After that they were able to pull him ashore.

The temple of Wat Sothom was built round the spot, and there he still sits to this day. People come by the thousands to pay homage to this deeply revered Luang Pho Sothon and beg him to grant their wishes – whether it is to cure their child or anything else urgently needed.

Rich and poor alike come. If you are in Thailand, why not go on any Sunday and see for yourself? You will find it a rich cultural experience to linger and watch the crowds from every stratum of Thai society come, worship Luang Pho Sothon, and take their leave. Wat Sothorn lies a mile or so outside Chachoengsao town towards the southwest. If you go by train or bus, a man-powered tricycle (*samlo*) will take you there. It makes a refreshing ride in the midday heat.

As you approach the large temple with its three identical, beautifully decorated porticos, you will hear the clash of cymbals and the plaintive song that accompanies classical dancers. Your *samlo* will set you down at the end of a narrow street of shops, and a stallholder will sell you a packet of three joss-sticks, flowers, a candle, and a square piece or two of gold leaf. Step inside the temple compound, mingle with the crowds and do as they do; take off your shoes, light your joss-sticks and candle, and kneel. Any glances you receive will be of warm approval and pleasure that a foreigner has come to join in worshipping at this much beloved place.

From time to time announcements over a loudspeaker give the names of those who have made donations to pay for a dance drama. Mats are laid down in the compound, and the young girl dancers, exquisite as flowers in their brilliantly sequined costumes, perform the short play. As in all Thai classical dancing, delicate and expressive hand and foot movements blend with the rhythm of their clear voices to the accompaniment of the tinkling *ranat*, resembling curved xylophones, and the clashing cymbals.

For a few baht you can have your own special dance drama performed in a wooden pavilion just outside the temple compound. The temple's daily income from donations, which always runs into five figures, is chalked up on a board inside. The money is used for flood relief and to build schools, hospitals and so on.

Inside the temple itself is an elegant group of twenty Buddha statues, continually being regilded with gold leaf applied by worshippers. At the back, towering over the other statues, Luang Pho Sothon sits serenely, his hands folded in his lap.

A walk of a few yards takes you down to the water's edge, where you can enjoy a cool drink and ponder over the sights and sounds you've seen, amid the sweet smell of incense, before making your way back to Bangkok.

Somewhere below *Luang Pho* are the gods and goddesses known as *Chao Pho* and *Chao Mae*. Perhaps a better English word for this class would be "spirits."

Among these are *Chao Pho* Prakan, the spirit of Death, who has a shrine at Lop Buri. Legend has it that the barn owl or screech owl is *Chao Pho* Prakan's emissary or messenger. If you hear this bird screeching as it flies over your home, watch the direction in which it is flying: if it is eastward, all is well, but if it is towards the west, death will come to someone in the household, for the setting sun symbolizes death.

Among goddesses, or *Chao Mae*, are two whom I shall deal with in Chapter 6 on Legends: *Chao Mae* Sammuk, the spirit of a girl who threw herself over a cliff near Bang Saen because of a broken heart, and *Chao Mae* Sao Hai, who appeared to villagers near Lop Buri in the guise of a log floating along the canal.

From time to time a news item mentions a visit by Their Majesties the King and Queen, perhaps with one of their royal children, to a provincial city to preside over a religious ceremony for anointing a newly erected city pillar replacing an old one damaged by the elements. The Thai name for such a pillar is *lak mueang*, defined in the dictionary as "the centre of the city, marked by a shrine dedicated to *Chao Pho* Lak Mueang or the guardian spirit of the city." Such a city pillar, then, is another example of a *Chao Pho*. It is also a guardian spirit – but one which protects an entire city, not just a single plot of land with a home or other building on it. The city pillar is also usually regarded as the city's foundation stone.

The best known city pillar in Thailand is that of Bangkok. It deserves a special section to itself.

## *Lak Mueang* – The Log That Helped to Found a City

Sukhothai . . . Ayutthaya . . . Bangkok . . . each of Thailand's capital cities has always had its own *"lak mueang"* or city pillar: the official city centre, marked by a shrine dedicated to *Phra* Lak Mueang, or the guardian spirit of the city, popularly known as *Chao Pho* Lak Mueang. The history of the *lak mueang* is colorful and interesting. Its roots lie in wars and victories. Like most countries the world over, Thailand's history has been much involved with wars against its neighbors, especially Burma, almost since time immemorial. In order to make sure of winning these wars, the commanders-in-chief of Thailand's armies (in the past, usually the reigning king) had to be expert in astrology. This was so that they could determine precisely the most auspicious day and hour to strike at the enemy, and the best strategy to use.

An important part of this strategy lay in boosting the morale of the Thai troops and lowering that of the enemy. This in turn was done by the correct tactical approach: The Thai soldiery must wear the proper "color of the day" – red for Sunday, yellow for Monday, pink for Tuesday and so on. (This is dealt with more fully in Chapter 8). But perhaps even more important were various essential astrological ceremonies, including one known as *tat mai khom nam*: "To disgrace the enemy in effigy before a battle in order to encourage one's own troops," according to the dictionary.

*Tat mai* means literally "to cut wood," and this was in fact done by the felling of a huge laburnum tree (*genus Cassia*).

The Thai name for this tree is *chaiyapruek*, or "the tree of success." This type of tree is scarce enough in Thailand; to find a really tall specimen is even more difficult. But a successful search was essential before each decisive battle was fought to ensure victory for the Thai armies. The resulting *chaiyapruek* log with its *prueksathewada*, or guardian spirit, inhabiting it, then became the city pillar (and hence, the foundation stone) of the victorious Thai capital.

After the Burmese sacking of Ayutthaya in 1767, General Chakri successfully routed the Burmese in a series of battles, thus enabling him to found the nation's present capital of Bangkok and assume the throne as King Rama I of the present Chakri Dynasty. The *chaiyapruek* which assured the final Thai victory on that occasion was over fifteen feet long. This sacred log thus became the City Pillar and foundation stone of Bangkok, in 1782.

A grand ceremony to set up the pillar, near where the Grand Palace would later be built, was held on April 21 that year. The log was embedded six-and-a-half feet deep in the ground and rose above the surface to a height of nine feet. At that time there was neither a building, nor even a roof, to protect it.

Thus the *prueksathewada*, or guardian spirit, in this mighty laburnum log which saved Bangkok from the Burmese has, so it is believed, been protecting not only the city itself and all who live in it, but the entire Thai nation for over two hundred years. For this reason it has always been venerated throughout the kingdom. King Chulalongkorn (Rama V) ordered the pillar rebuilt and a *mondop*, or pavilion with a spire, built to house it. This was the occasion for another grand celebration, at which a proclamation was issued inviting all the spirits and gods to come and inhabit the pillar in order to protect the city and her people.

This shrine does not figure on the average tourist's or visitor's itinerary, but it is certainly well worth a visit. It lies at the southeast corner of the Phramane Grounds or Sanam Luang, very near the corner of the outside wall of the Grand Palace grounds. It is from the City Pillar that all road distances to points throughout the country are measured.

There are now five images of spirit-gods inside the shrine, four of them cast in solid gold. *Chao Pho* Lak Mueang's favorite food is said to be hard-boiled eggs, and like some other gods, this spirit also enjoys Thai classical dancing. All members of the Thai public who come here to pay homage do so in order to ask for a wish to be fulfilled, whether it is a pregnant woman who prays for a baby boy, someone who desperately wants their ailing mother to recover, or whatever else we mortals usually wish for: Gains, honors, and so on. The best time to ask for favors is before eleven a.m., after which *Chao Pho* Lak Mueang is believed to retire to heaven for the rest of the day. So a special dance performance is put on for him every day between ten and eleven a.m. After that, classical dance dramas for the public continue for the rest of the day until four p.m.

The scene at the Lak Mueang shrine is very colorful indeed. You can stay and watch classical dancing all day long if you want, and mingle with crowds from every walk of Thai life. After watching the dancing and the classical *piphat* band with its *khong wong yai*, or semi-circular set of graded gongs, *ranat*, or curved xylophone, and drums, have a look inside the inner part of the shrine to see the pillar itself, with its steady stream of worshippers. Joss-sticks are incessantly lit, flower garlands are offered in thanks for some wish granted, gold leaf is reverently applied to the pillar . . . It is a sight one should not miss.

# Traditional Thai Medicine

The taxi driver, though young, was gloomy and obviously felt tired. Suddenly he stopped outside a drugstore, muttered in Thai "Shan't be a moment," and entered the shop. A minute later he emerged with a small bottle, less than half a pint in size. He sat down in his driver's seat and drained the contents at a single gulp. The effect was almost like magic. Like Popeye with his spinach, the young man seemed to swell visibly. A gleam appeared in his eye and a smile on his face. Tossing the empty bottle on the floor beside him, he drove on.

Curious, I picked the bottle up. Examining the label, I saw a drawing of a turnip-like root with lots of hairs and fibers sprouting from the end, as if it needed a shave rather badly. The caption, in both Thai and English, said: "Korea Tang Gui Jup – for increasing vitality." The driver, by now grinning cheerfully, said he usually drank two or three bottles a week because he suffered from lack of energy (a fairly common complaint which I for one share!). He found this particular herbal medicine helped him tremendously – as indeed the dramatic change in his face and manner showed quite clearly.

Later I discovered the root shown on the label was ginseng. This is said to come from only two places: Pusan in Korea, and Manchuria. How much truth there is in that, I do not know. At the time, I was told by a pharmacologist that a single big root, about one meter long, could cost anything from six thousand to ten thousand baht.

This incident with the taxi driver illustrates the fact that traditional herbal medicine is still very much alive in Thailand. A large section of the population uses it regularly in one form or another. Two basic kinds are recognized here:

Thai and Chinese. The main difference seems to be that the Thai variety is on the whole milder and slower-acting, while the Chinese aims at a quick, sharp cure. Also, Thai medicines are usually sold in crude form for making up at home, whereas Chinese are sold already steamed and chopped.

Every village throughout Thailand has its own local practitioner of traditional medicine. He is usually a respected village elder or a monk. Prescriptions vary from region to region; in the South, for instance, a plant called *salet phangphon*, or "mongoose saliva," is used against snake-bite. The plant is pounded to a pulp and soaked in alcohol or some other liquid. The decoction is drunk, and the solid matter is used as a poultice.

If you are interested in medicinal herbs, you might enjoy a browse round Chao Krom Poe, one of Bangkok's main retailers. The shop is at 229 Chakkrawat Road, right next to the entrance to Wat Chakkrawat. As you go in, you will smell the fragrant, spicy smell of herbalists' shops everywhere. This shop stocks over a thousand herbs – some local, others from India, China, Korea, and Indonesia.

Although some superstition still surrounds the lore and practice of herbal medicine in Thailand as it does elsewhere, nevertheless there is no doubt that in the hands of Thailand's thousands of experts they are very effective in curing many diseases.

The history of their use in this country goes back a long time. Like many Thai traditions and customs, the use of herbal medicines hailed originally from India, where they were known even before the Buddha's time twenty-five hundred years ago. I am grateful to Joseph Sribuapan, a blind Thai masseur, for the following history of ancient traditional medicines and the equally ancient skill of traditional massage, which have always gone hand-in-hand.

At the Indian town of Taxila a great academy of learning was founded by Rokha Marutin. Kings and rich men sent their sons to learn all kinds of skills such as the martial and fine arts, and medicine which included as two of its branches herbal medicine and massage. A pupil of Rokha Marutin named Jivaka Komarabaccha (Thai: Chiwok Komaraphat) became the Buddha's medical adviser.

India was a very progressive country, and word of the Taxila Academy spread to China, whose Emperor sent his doctors to study there. Amongst other techniques, they learnt the "touch" method, in which the patient's ailment is diagnosed by touching the middle of his palm – rather as a modern doctor takes a patient's pulse, except that the physicians of old could tell simply from touching the palm everything that was wrong and not just the pulse rate.

When the Chinese Emperor fell sick, he sent for Rokha Marutin, who cured him and other ailing Chinese by a combination of herbal medicine and massage. Before leaving India for China, Rokha Marutin had handed over his Academy, with all its store of knowledge, to his pupil Jivaka, who kept all the old skills alive. Rokha Marutin remained in China and never returned to India, but the fame of the Academy which he founded spread as far as Egypt, whose rulers invited Jivaka to go there and teach them herbal medicine.

Later the Academy disappeared, but its ancient medical knowledge, particularly herbal medicine and massage, survived through individual teachers. The first Buddhist monks to reach Thailand, as well as Brahmins and traveling merchants, brought these skills and knowledge with them to this country, where today they are known collectively as *ya samunphrai*. Once it reached Thailand, the knowledge of these two branches of medicine – herbal medicine and traditional massage – gradually spread, and both of them became very popular as cures for all kinds of aches and pains. Their popularity reached a peak at about the beginning of the present Chakri Dynasty over two hundred years ago. After that, interest apparently waned, and some of the centuries-old secrets died with their practitioners, who during their lifetime had been unwilling to share them with their competitors.

King Nangklao (Rama III) realised the danger of the entire tradition being lost for ever, and took steps to prevent this from happening. He summoned together all the traditional medicine practitioners still living, obtained from them all the available store of knowledge about herbal medicine and massage, and had it inscribed on marble tablets, which were placed on the walls of verandahs throughout Wat Pho (the Temple of the Reclining Buddha), where the inscriptions can still be seen today.

Later public interest flagged once again, until it was once more revived by a later Chakri monarch, King Vajiravudh (Rama VI). Like his predecessor, he too assembled all the practicing doctors, and the organization known today as the Association of Schools for Ancient Medicine was established. First situated in Wat Thepthida, it gave rise to a second association with the same aims based at Wat Pho. The original association at Wat Thepthida later outgrew its quarters and moved across the street to Wat Parinayok, where it functions today, training new doctors and masseurs in the ancient and very effective medical skills handed down from India.

I have been told there are now five schools of traditional medicine in Bangkok. Their object is to prevent the skills still known from dying out. In the provinces, their place is taken by apprenticeship with a known and capable teacher, who hands his knowledge on.

The set of three botanical-medical textbooks used and sold by the two medical schools at Wat Pho and Wat Parinayok are, of course, printed entirely in Thai apart from the Latin botanical name of each plant, which is given in Western characters. The books contain drawings of many interesting-looking plants.

The curative properties attributed by the books to some of the plants cover a wide spectrum of complaints. Here are a few examples chosen at random.

The root of the herb *rauwolfia*, known locally as *rayom*, is claimed to reduce high blood pressure, get rid of intestinal worms, and act as a tranquillizer and appetite stimulator. It is also used in veterinary work.

*Apocynaceae*, or *chalut khao*, is a climbing creeper useful in general medicine. Remove the bark, pound the inside, and dry it in the sun until it turns white. It gives off a strong smell; boil it in water and it can be used to make incense, while the leaves and berries can cure fever. The flowers can cure delirium, hiccough, and stomach pains, and improve blood circulation.

*Palmae, nipa fructicans,* or *chak* has leaves with astringent properties. It can cure diarrhea and wind, phlegm, and various other body poisons. Sugar made from the fruit can also cure piles. This is the same *nipa* plant which is used to build houses and thatch roofs.

In the hands of skilled practitioners these traditional herbal medicines are highly effective. To give just one example, an acquaintance of mine went on a car trip to Khao Yai with a qualified herbal medicine practitioner. This man had long suffered from car sickness, especially on twisty roads – and that road to Khao Yai is very twisty indeed. Luckily his herbal medicine friend had brought along a bottle of *ya hom* ("pleasant-smelling medicine") containing some thirty-six different ingredients. This cured my acquaintance's sickness immediately.

And now for the technique of traditional massage, as related to me by the blind Thai masseur, Joseph Sribuapan.

Joseph is a calm, confident man in spite of his blindness. He speaks passably good English, and his blind wife speaks it fluently. He hails from Chaiyaphum Province in the Northeast. At the age of eight Joseph's education was abruptly halted when a fever left him blind. He spent the next four years at home, and it was at this time that he first became interested in massage.

Middle-aged men in Thailand, especially upcountry, often ask a younger member of the family, say a child of eight or ten, to give them a rudimentary sort of massage. This consists in the child walking up and down the older person's back, and squeezing, kneading, and pinching his arms and legs. Although crude, this form of massage is apparently quite effective in relaxing the muscles, stimulating the circulation and removing tiredness. Anyway, Joseph's uncle often asked his blind young nephew to give him this kind of massage; and the idea took root in the little boy's mind, to surface again many years later.

When he was thirteen, Joseph came to Bangkok to study at the School for the Blind. He learned to read and write in Braille, and to do canework, basketry, and other handicrafts. Later he himself became a teacher at the Blind School in Chiang Mai, after which he returned to Bangkok to study advanced handicrafts at the training centre for the blind at Pak Kret, just north of the city. Here he learned leatherwork, carpentry, metal work, and how to make cement tiles and fence poles.

After that, he and his wife tried their hand at chicken farming for a time, but it didn't work out. Finally a friend told

Joseph about the Association of Schools for Traditional Medicine at Wat Parinayok, where the ancient massage technique is also taught. This brought back Joseph's childhood memories of walking up and down on his prostrate uncle, so he went to the school, where he received full and proper training in this rather esoteric skill.

With the manual dexterity typical of the blind, Joseph picked up the technique fairly easily, and by dint of.hard work he managed to complete the normally three-year course in only one year. At first he practiced so hard that he got blisters on all his fingers and thumbs at once!

Traditional massage helps to stimulate blood circulation by the application of hand pressure at certain key points of the body. Diagrams showing these key spots are engraved on stone slabs at Wat Pho, like the herbal medicine prescriptions I referred to earlier. Good circulation in turn helps towards improved health.

In my own case, I asked for Joseph's help on two separate occasions. The first time was at home, not long after I had begun practicing meditation and was suffering agonies from trying to sit cross-legged for the first time in over sixty years. I asked Joseph whether he could do anything to ease the aches in my legs and back. For over two hours Joseph gave me the works – pushing, prodding, twisting, squeezing and doing his best to snap off both my legs at the knees. He shook his head sadly.

"Your left leg isn't as good as your right one," he said politely. How true he spoke. It is always my left foot which goes numb before the right one, whenever I am meditating. The two-hour treatment, painful though it was, certainly helped my cross-legged problem, as did the weekly hot poultice made of mashed lily leaves from the garden which Joseph showed my wife how to make and apply.

The second time I needed Joseph's help was during my brief spell as a monk. An old backache returned (probably due to subconsciously walking with one shoulder higher than the other to prevent my robe slipping off). Joseph came to my *kuti*, or monk's dwelling, and the pressure from his strong thumbs in the right places soon did away with the trouble.

Joseph has told me a few other ways in which traditional massage in various special forms can help to alleviate sickness. Combined with certain special herbs it can soften the veins. It can reduce high fever and epileptic fits, and it can stop convulsions caused by falls, which would otherwise result in paralysis. It can help in treating the early stages of other forms of paralysis, can straighten a crooked mouth, and help patients who are dumb, and those with speech defects.

Every day at Wat Samphya (the Temple of the Three Peers) in Banglamphu you may see patients being treated for paralysis by this time-honored twenty-five hundred-year-old technique of traditional massage.

## Preserving Thailand's Traditional Arts of Self-Defense

"About six to seven hundred years ago the people of Thailand defended themselves from their enemies with various weapons and the art of using these weapons has been handed down to the present generation.

"The weapons consist mainly of straight swords, curved swords, daggers, arm protectors, lances, halberds, spears, and sticks. Great skill was required and long periods of training went into the preparation of a good warrior. Speed and ability were of prime importance and trainees were well versed in Thai-style boxing, judo, and dancing, as well as sword and dagger fighting.

"After Thailand became united as a nation and there were periods of peace, the people continued to practice the use of weapons, and their use become a national sport.

"These games become known as the "*krabi-krabong* games" and were performed before foreign guests and during important ceremonies. To add more color and interest to these games, music was played during the performances. The musical instruments consisted of two Indian drums, one Javanese pipe, and a set of cymbals."

Those words come from a leaflet issued by the "Samnak Dap Phutthaisawan," or Buddhai Sawan Sword-Fighting Institute. I found the story of this institute, which I came across by accident, very interesting and typically Thai.

A friend kindly arranged for me to meet Mr. Samai Mesamana, the institute's founder, owner and headmaster all rolled into one. Mr. Samai came along with another of the institute's instructors, Mr. Chalong Phanphet, a specialist in the art of fixing the *mongkhon*, or special head-dress worn during sword-fighting. At first glance I took both men to be somewhere between forty-five and fifty; they were sprightly and obviously in the best of health. Shortly afterwards I discovered that Mr. Samai was actually sixty-five – quite the most robust-looking and vigorous man of that age I had met for a long time. And Mr. Chalong was fifty-five.

Mr. Samai told me his forbears were royal knights of old who served the kings of Ayutthaya, and that this fact was the reason for his interest in reviving the traditional Thai arts of sword-fighting and self-defense.

The institute's name is taken from the Buddhaisawan

Temple in Ayutthaya, which was built in 1353 A.D. by King U-thong, founder of the first Ayutthaya Dynasty, on the site of the palace where he lived before establishing the new capital. This was the first temple in Thailand to teach knights and the children of royalty the skills of sword-fighting. At that time it was also Thailand's largest temple, and its abbot was the Supreme Patriarch, *Somdet Phra* Phutthachan. The ruins of the Buddhaisawan Temple can still be seen today, including the original Supreme Patriarch's *kuti*, or dwelling, and his alms-bowl and robes, preserved by the Fine Arts Department.

Mr. Samai also hailed from Ayutthaya. After graduating in Physical Education from Suan Kularb School in Bangkok and working in various jobs for ten years or so, he felt the need to revive the ancient arts of his ancestors. Together with a few kindred spirits, he founded the Buddhai Sawan Sword-Fighting Society, and as such it remained for its first ten years. That was more than forty-five years ago. As interest in the movement spread and as the group became larger, it became necessary under law to register it as a school, and so the institute came into being, and has been flourishing for many years. Mr. Samai believed it was the first such school in Thailand.

Mr. Samai made himself an expert and specialist in the finer details of traditional Thai sword-fighting, and today the institute trains adults and children from all walks of life in the age-old arts of self-defense and the allied tradition of classical dance. The institute's main objectives are to equip students with skills in self-defense against all types of weapons, from fists to guns; to enable them to become good soldiers; to turn out graduates who are qualified teachers, able to pass on this skill to others; and to preserve Thailand's old traditions of sword-fighting and classical dancing to help develop the country.

Training in sword-fighting is given to people from all walks of life, especially soldiers and policemen, but also university, college, and school students. Several different courses are offered, full-time and part-time (at weekends and during holidays). The courses last six months, a year, or two years, and include Thai boxing as well as international methods of self-defense such as judo. "Our students must be able to defend themselves against attackers using improvised weapons found in the home, such as knives, sticks, and even pens," said Mr. Samai.

Part of each course involves training in the actual making of swords and other traditional weapons. Diplomas are awarded to those who pass the institute's examinations successfully, and all students who pass the one-year or two-year course are found jobs as teachers by the institute; those with the highest grades are taken on by the institute itself as instructors.

One might imagine that only mock wooden swords are used in instruction and practice. This is in fact the case during the first three months' training only; after that, real, razor-sharp weapons are used. This makes students more careful, said Mr. Samai. But with these weapons, absolute 100 percent unwavering concentration is also essential to avoid harming one's "opponent," or being wounded oneself. And this high degree of concentration is achieved in the age-old, proven way: By meditation, at the beginning and end of every day's instruction.

All students also take an oath on entering the institute for training never to lie to their parents, teachers, or anyone else, and never to quarrel amongst themselves or harbor ill-feeling of any kind towards one another. Abiding by this oath, and with the help of the twice-daily meditation period, the students are able to maintain the necessary concentration and cool headedness (or as the Thais say, a cool heart). Mr. Samai pointed to the effectiveness of this method: Nobody at the institute ever gets hurt!

Mr. Samai and his troupe have performed at the National Theatre before His Majesty the King, and a special performance was put on at Wat Kasatrathirat in Ayutthaya for Britain's Queen Elizabeth and Prince Philip in 1972. His Majesty the King has also granted royal recognition to the institute and presented it with a special emblem.

The institute works closely with the Tourism Authority of Thailand, through which it has given performances almost all over the world, whenever Thai arts and culture are on display. During March and April, Thai students at the institute are joined by young Americans, Australians, and other foreigners.

## Telling the Time

I wonder how many Westerners have had experiences similar to the one I had during my early days in Thailand. A Thai friend, whose English was not very good (but better than my Thai, which was virtually non-existent), said to me on the phone, "you can telephone me any day at about three o'clock in the morning – but don't leave it until four o'clock, or I may have gone out."

I was a bit bewildered, but being a stranger to these parts I thought perhaps they did keep unusual hours here. It was only considerably later, when I had learned the language, that I realised he had been referring to NINE o'clock and TEN o'clock in the morning!

In colloquial Thai you can say either *sam mong chao* (which translated word for word does mean "three o'clock in the morning") or *kao mong chao* (which means "nine o'clock in the morning"). What my friend had done, of course, was to translate the first of these two versions directly, but incorrectly, into English. Since then I have heard others make similar mistakes; maybe the same has happened to readers, too.

The colloquial Thai system of telling the time of day is very old. In fact, a variety of systems is used. The most common system divides the twenty-four-hour day into four periods of six hours each. In this system the wee small hours are prefaced by *ti*, meaning "to strike." Thus one a.m. is *ti nueng*, two a.m. *ti song*, and so on. So if I had been able to speak Thai I could have asked my friend if he really meant *ti sam* (three a.m.) and *ti si* (four a.m.). But my Thai at that time was limited more or less to *sawatdi khrap*, and even then no one understood me.

The *ti* period goes up to *ti hok* (six a.m.), at which time it comes to an end and the next period takes over. In fact there is an overlap, and six a.m. is more commonly known as *hok mong chao*. It is also occasionally known as *yam rung*. *Mong* means the hour of the clock during daytime, and *chao* means "morning." From now on, further confusion sets in for the foreigner along the lines of my little anecdote above.

Seven a.m. can be either *nueng mong chao* (literally, "one o'clock in the morning") or *chet mong chao* (*chet* is seven). This clock double-speak goes on all the way to eleven a.m., which may be either *ha mong chao* ("five o'clock in the morning") or *sip-et mong chao* ("eleven o'clock in the morning").

Midday is *thiang wan*, literally "day-noon." (Occasionally *yam thiang*). We are in the clear for the next two hours: One p.m. is *bai mong*; *bai*, referring to the sun, means "to decline," so it also means "afternoon." Two p.m. is *bai song mong*. There are no alternative forms.

But by three p.m. evening already starts rearing its rather premature and confusing head: This hour can either follow logically after its predecessor, being called *bai sam mong*, or it can be *sam mong yen* – "three o'clock in the evening," an expression surely more suited to the dark winter days of lands in the far north such as Britain. Similarly, four p.m. can be either *bai si mong* or *si mong yen*, but the latter is far more common. And by five p.m., evening has really set in, even though the sun is still streaming down mercilessly out of a clear blue sky; five p.m. is *ha mong yen* – five o'clock in the evening, and nothing else.

One more yen to go. Six p.m. is *hok mong yen* (also known as *yam kham*). After that, the drum starts banging: the old time drum known as *thum* used for striking the night hours. Thus, seven p.m. is *nueng thum* (or sometimes the other way round, *thum nueng*). Eight p.m. is *song thum*, nine p.m. is *sam thum*, ten p.m. *see thum*, and eleven p.m. *ha thum*. There are again no alternative forms during this six hour stretch. Midnight, logically enough, is *thiang khuen* ("night-noon,") or *song yam*.

The words *ti, mong, thum,* and *yam* originated in the palace from the sounds of the drums, gongs, and bells which were used to mark the hours.

So that's it. Like most things in life, once you get to know the colloquial Thai system of telling the time, it isn't as confusing as it first seems. You can often hear conversations between Thai people in which both forms are used with equal frequency – *sam mong chao* and *kao mong chao*, for instance.

This chronicle of the times would not be complete without mention of a rather rare and ancient, but still used, three-hourly system. This uses the word *yam*, meaning a watchman or sentry, which was formerly used to mark the chang-ing of the palace guards. In this system, there are eight periods of three hours each. A friend tells me this form is now met mainly in novels of olden times and the like.

The reason I have stressed the colloquial form of telling the time is that it is, of course, not the "official" system. It would never work for train times, radio programmes, or – heaven help us – airline schedules! So in Thailand, as in nearly every country I suppose, there is also a formal system using the standard twenty-four-hour clock starting at midnight, or "zero-zero, zero-zero hours," in which two a.m. becomes the rather military-sounding "0200 hours." and two p.m. is "1400 hours." In Thai, this system uses the word *nalika*, meaning "a clock."

Try dialing what used to be called the "speaking clock," or TIM in my younger days in Britain; the Bangkok number is 181. You will hear the recorded Thai equivalent of the "girl with the golden voice," as she was known in pre-war Britain, saying clearly and sweetly, "at the next stroke it will be precisely *sipchet nalika, sip-song nathi, yisip winathi* (17.12 and 20 seconds) .... BEEP!... At the next stroke it will be precisely ..."

Happy listening!

## Lunar Months

If you thought the Thai system of telling the time which I described in the last section is a bit complicated, the names of the calendar months by contrast follow a beautifully simple system. Here they are:

| January | - | Mokkarakhom |
| February | - | Kumphaphan |

| | | |
|---|---|---|
| March | - | Minakhom |
| April | - | Mesayon |
| May | - | Phrutsaphakhom |
| June | - | Mithunayon |
| July | - | Karakadakhom |
| August | - | Singhakhom |
| September | - | Kanyayon |
| October | - | Tulakhom |
| November | - | Phrutsachikayon |
| December | - | Thanwakhom |

Can you follow the pattern? The key lies in the endings. The months with thirty days – April, June, September and November- all end in *-yon*. All the rest, with thirty-one days, end in *-khom*, with the solitary exception of February, which with twenty-eight days has an ending unlike all the others: *-phan*.

Perhaps you remember the old English rhyme about this, which went: "Thirty days hath September, April, June, and dull November; all the rest have thirty-one, excepting February alone, which hath but twenty-eight days clear, and twenty-nine in each Leap Year." We children had to memorize that in kindergarten, but how complicated it seems compared with the Thai system, in which every man, woman, and child knows instantly from the ending, *-yon* or *-khom*, just how many days there are in each month!

Now, having lured you on with that delightfully simple system, let me with fiendish glee confuse you utterly. We shall now discuss the lunar system of months and days of the month, adopted centuries ago by the Thais from the Chinese. These are based on the phases of the moon, and they probably didn't seem so complicated in earlier times before the Western-style calendar months and seven-day week were introduced, when an attempt was presumably made to make the two systems compatible.

A complete cycle of the moon, from new moon to full moon and back to new again, takes twenty-nine and one half days. So alternate lunar months have to be thirty days long and twenty-nine days long. The even-numbered months have thirty days (fifteen days of waxing moon and fifteen days of waning); the odd-numbered months have twenty-nine days (fifteen days waxing, fourteen days waning).

In Thai, "waxing" is *kheun*, and "waning" is *raem*. You can see the lunar dates printed in Thai script on most Thai calendars and diaries; June 19, 1978 was *khuen* 14 *kham duean* 7, literally, "waxing fourteen nights, month seven," for instance.

But surely June is the sixth month – not the seventh? Yes – the sixth calendar month. And we're now talking about lunar months.

The trouble with fitting lunar months into the calendar year is that they are shorter than the calendar months; the twelve calendar months add up exactly to 365 days, whereas a little arithmetic shows that twelve lunar months, of thirty and twenty-nine days alternately, only amount to 354 days. So there's a difference of eleven days, and over a period of years the lunar months gradually creep ahead of the calendar months. Most years seem to start off with January 1 being somewhere in the second lunar month.

To overcome this difficulty, a cunning ruse is resorted to: From time to time an EXTRA eighth lunar month is shoved in, so that the two eighth lunar months extend from June to August. This system must surely be very ancient indeed, because after all it is the earth's motion round the sun that makes the year 365 days long, and as far as I know, that has not changed for millions of years – except, of course, for Leap Year.

I decided to try and find out just how often the extra eighth month was inserted into the year. This proved difficult, because nobody seemed to have the faintest idea. Then my wife had a brainwave; she looked it up in her One-hundred-year astrological calendar. She came up with two groups of years with "double-eighth" lunar months, one taken at random round about World War I, and the other during the current period. I have translated them from Buddhist Era years into A.D. by subtracting 543 (the difference between the Buddhist and Christian Eras). Here they are years in which there were TWO eighth lunar months: 1912, 1915, 1918, 1920, 1923; and 1972, 1975, 1977, 1980, 1983, 1985. The intervals, in numbers of years, between these years are: 3, 3, 2, 3, and 3, 2, 3, 3, 2. Check? OK! So the pattern in which the "double-eighth" years are spaced out seems to be two intervals of three years each, followed by one interval of two years, then repeat. Phew!

The lunar calendar is still used in rural Thailand, especially in the Northeast and in the more remote villages. In this system the days of the week are reckoned by the Buddhist holy days or *wan phra*, literally, "monks' days." These fall on the eighth and fifteenth waxing-moon days (the latter being *wan phen*, the day of the full moon), and the eighth and fifteenth waning-moon days (the fourteenth in odd-numbered months), the latter being the day of the new moon.

During my wife's childhood and adolescence in the late 1940s and 1950s, she and her grandmother cared little about Sunday, Monday, Tuesday, and so on. But her grandmother, being a devout Buddhist, always remembered exactly when each *wan phra* was due. She also knew which lunar month it was, and what is more, she somehow managed to keep count of the years as well, and always knew when it was time for those two eighth months!

Even today, wall calendars of the commercial type include details of each day giving the lunar month and the exact phase of the waxing or waning moon; *wan phra* days are marked by a picture of the Buddha superimposed on the calendar date. At the early morning start of each day's radio programme, too, the same information is given.

During most of the year, only the first two *wan phra* in each lunar month are observed by most rural people. My wife can remember taking bags of rice every month on those two days to Wat Suan Som (the Orange Grove Temple) near her home, so that the monks would not need to go out on their early-morning alms round on these special days. During the three rainy months of *Phansa* or Lent, from July to October, all four *wan phra* days in each month are often observed.

The complex and very Thai relationship between the lunar and solar calendars is discussed further in the chapter "How dates are reckoned" in the companion volume to this book, *More Thai Ways*.

A good many years ago the cinema boardings in Bangkok were plastered with advertisements for a film called *Sao Ha*, literally "Saturday Five," although the English title was "The Great Saturday." I did not see the film and I have no idea what it was about, but I did find out what the title means.

"Saturday Five" is when the *fifth* day of the waxing (or waning) moon of the *fifth* lunar month falls on a Saturday. No one seems to know the significance of this, but anyway such a Saturday occurs rather seldom and spasmodically, so it is considered a lucky, auspicious and powerful day. Hence its English title, "The Great Saturday." It occurred in 1960,

1970, 1973, and on 5th April 1980 – there was a seven-year gap between the last two.

Each time a "Saturday Five" comes round, people take their Buddha images to certain temples and leave them there overnight. At Wat Sadet in Pathum Thani, I was told there were a thousand or more householders' Buddha images on that night in 1973. The monks chanted at night, blessing all the images. At some other temples new images were cast.

If a "Saturday Five" occurs in the fifth year of the twelve-year cycle as well, that makes it even more powerful and lucky. So, now to the twelve year cycle.

## The Twelve-Year Cycle

Like the lunar months, the twelve-year cycle originally came to Thailand from China. Westerners familiar with this country will already know how important the completion of a twelve year cycle is. Whether it is the 12th anniversary of a company, or a person's 24th, 36th, 48th, 60th, 72nd, or even 84th birthday, it is an auspicious occasion for celebration and rejoicing. (I myself passed my "seventh-cycle" or, 84th birthday several years ago.)

Each year in the twelve-year cycle is associated with a different animal. Each year also has its special Thai name though I have not been able to find out where these names have come from. (A friend believes they are from Sanskrit and Pali.) Anyway, here they are. (*Pi* means "year").

| YEAR NUMBER | THE YEAR OF THE | THAI NAME |
|---|---|---|
| 1 | Rat | *Pi Chuat* |
| 2 | Ox | *Pi Chalu* |

| 3 | Tiger | *Pi Khan* |
|---|---|---|
| 4 | Rabbit | *Pi Thao* |
| 5 | Sea-serpent | *Pi Marong* |
| 6 | Small snake | *Pi Maseng* |
| 7 | Horse | *Pi Mamia* |
| 8 | Goat | *Pi Mamae* |
| 9 | Monkey | *Pi Wok* |
| 10 | Cock | *Pi Raka* |
| 11 | Dog | *Pi Cho* |
| 12 | Pig | *Pi Kun* |

Each year has its own "element" – water, earth, wood, gold, fire, or iron – its own guardian spirit, and its own "type of being."

There is a huge 650-page book called *"Phrommachat,"* which means something like "Brahma-life" or "Brahma Birth." The subheading says: "An anthology of folk mythology and fortune-telling." It is an absolute mine of information. The book sets out the general characteristics of those born in each of the twelve years.

Here, much abbreviated, is what the book says about Year One, the Year of the Rat:

Anyone born in the Year of the Rat is a "male deity" whose element is water. The guardian spirit lives in a coconut or banana tree. The Sun rules the mouth, and the person's speech will be bold and decisive, suitable for conversing with nobles or those of high military rank. The Moon and Mercury govern the hands, so he will be incapable of delicate handicraft work. Saturn rules the heart, so he is indecisive, easily influenced by others for good or evil.

The feet are ruled by Jupiter and Saturn, and such a person enjoys foreign travel. If a man, he is dogged by bad luck when young but will be blessed with good fortune and power later on. If a woman, she will tend to suffer from illness and will be unlucky as far as husbands are concerned.

A person born in the fifth, sixth, or seventh (lunar) month of the Year of the Rat is a "white-bellied rat" bearing a jewel. His element is sea-water. He is intelligent, but weak-willed, will prosper in government service and have elephants, horses, and freeman attendants. If a farmer or businessman, he will also become wealthy.

Someone born in the eighth, ninth, or tenth month is a "house rat," whose element is canal-water, and he will encounter hardship. Unsuitable for government service, he will just about make it as a farmer. Born in the eleventh, twelfth, or first month, a person is a "pygmy shrew" (also a type of rat), and is sinful by nature. A person born in the second, third, or fourth month is a "field rat" who will succeed in farming or business and will have many children.

A person born in Year Two, the Year of the Ox, or *Pi Chalu*, is a "male human" whose guardian spirit lives in the sugar-palm tree. His life-span is governed by Brahma's mouth, his speech by the Moon; bold and shrewd of speech, he understands philosophy well. The heart is governed by Mercury, which also makes him clever and quick to grasp new ideas. If a man, he will have several wives and enjoy flirting with girls. If a woman, she will probably be divorced.

Born in the Year of the Tiger – *Pi Khan* – a person is a "female sea-ogre" whose guardian spirit lives in the turmeric plant. My wife is a "tiger." Upcountry, she says, after a baby is born the placenta or afterbirth is put in an earthen pot and buried under the tree or plant in which the relevant guardian spirit lives – in her case, therefore, a turmeric plant.

The tiger is, of course, a fierce and powerful animal, which can dominate weaker animals such as the pig. My wife's son was born in the Year of the Pig, and it is a fact that he is a docile boy who has always obeyed his mum. (A tiger can also dominate a rabbit. I am a "rabbit" ... But let us leave it at that, shall we?) A male "tiger" is likely to brag about girls, crack jokes, and generally act in a carefree way. A woman "tiger" is likely to have two husbands (true again in my wife's case!).

As I just said, I was born in the Year of the Rabbit, *Pi Thoa*. A "rabbit" is a "female human" whose guardian spirit lives in the *nalike* coconut or red cotton tree. A friend of my wife's is a "rabbit" and her son is a "pig." The pig is stronger than the rabbit, and again it is true that this woman simply cannot control or discipline her son.

A "rabbit's" mouth, governed by Mercury, gives him an unfortunate turn of speech so that he cannot persuade other people to his own way of thinking. The hand is governed by Jupiter and Saturn, and he is neat and tidy. (I do not think this really applies to me!)

The Year of the Sea-Serpent, *Pi Marong*, brings the characteristics of a "male deity," whose guardian spirit lives in the bamboo plant or red cotton tree. His heart, governed by Saturn, makes him quick to anger but just as quick to forget again.

A "small snake," one born in *Pi Maseng*, is a "male human" whose guardian spirit lives in the bamboo plant and *rang* tree. Before setting out to seek his fortune, he should first inform these trees; he will then receive vast wealth and great good fortune.

A "horse," born in 1978 (*Pi Mamia*), or anyone whose age that year was twelve or a multiple of twelve such as twenty-four, thirty-six, and so on, is a "female deity" whose guardian spirit lives in the *takien* and banana trees. His mouth, governed by Saturn, makes him arrogant in both speech and deed.

A "goat," born in *Pi Mamae*, is also a "female-deity" whose guardian spirit lives in the *parichat*, a kind of flowering tree, or in the wild bamboo. The heart is governed by Mars and he enjoys acquiring knowledge. A woman born in this year is likely to have several husbands.

A "monkey," born in *Pi Wok*, is a "male sea-ogre" whose guardian spirit lives in the jackfruit tree. Conceited in speech, he is nevertheless a favorite with the nobility.

A "cock," born in *Pi Raka*, is again a "male sea-ogre" whose guardian spirit lives in the rubber tree and cotton plant. The mouth is under Mars, and his speech is curt.

A "dog," born in *Pi Cho*, is a "female sea-ogre" with a guardian spirit living in the cassava tree and the *bua bok*, a kind of lotus. He tends to suffer from worms, and may have a scar on his face.

Last in the twelve year cycle is *Pi Kun*, the Year of the Pig. A "pig" is a "female human" whose guardian spirit lives in the lotus plant. He is quick-tempered and impatient.

My wife says, logically enough, that if the animal corresponding to a man's "birth-year" is stronger than that of his wife, he will be able to control her. The best possible marriage, she says is between a "male human" husband and a "female human" wife. For instance, if the husband is an "ox" and the wife a "rabbit," the marriage will be prosperous, happy, and long-lasting.

To end with, here is a thought for the ladies. If you do not want to reveal your age (and with all gallantry, I have met very few ladies who do!), don't tell anyone which "animal" you are. They can easily work out your age (to the nearest twelve years!) from the twelve-year cycle.

But nicknames such as "Nu" ("Rat") or "Phae" ("Goat") can sometimes give the game away. A Thai friend was once trying to find out a girl's age, which she refused to tell him.

But her nickname was "Mu" ("Pig") and he guessed (correctly) that this was because she was actually born in the Year of the Pig. After a moment's calculation, he announced (again correctly) that she was twenty-two – rather to her astonishment!

## When a Child is Born

My wife Laddawan's mother died when Laddawan was only a year old and her sister was two. So she does not know for certain whether her mother underwent the post-natal treatment known as *yu fai*, literally "staying by the fire," but it seems very likely that this was so. At least one of her five aunts went through this procedure after giving birth to each of her children.

In common with most of the customs and lore I have learnt from my wife, this habit whereby a woman is kept near a hot fire up to seven days after giving birth dates back to days gone by when there were few, if any, rural doctors and expert knowledge about herbal remedies was not easy to come by. The purpose of *yu fai*, which I believe is still carried out in many rural areas of Thailand, is to help the mother regain her strength after giving birth. It may only be done if the baby has been delivered by a midwife. Here is a rough description of this procedure.

Members of the family prepare a kind of temporary camp bed or litter called a *mae krae*, made of bamboo stems with banana-tree trunks chopped in half and placed on top. The spaces between the trunks are filled with earth to retain the heat inside the bed and to prevent the surroundings from becoming too hot. The charcoal stove which provides the heat is also insulated by standing it on a large slice of banana-trunk. Preparation of both bed and stove must be carefully timed so as to be ready just when they are needed, but not before, because that would be unlucky.

Other preparations for the *yu fai* ceremony include massive protection of the mother against evil spirits. Special pieces of cloth with magic charms drawn on them are hung around the bed at the eight points of the compass and on the ceiling and floor. Thorns of the *phutsa* tree, or of tamarind or bamboo, all of which can easily be found growing wild, are placed underneath the room and stuffed into every hole and crack in the house to stop spirits entering. The sacred white *sat sin* cord, previously blessed by monks, is also draped around the room; no evil spirit can cross this thread.

A symbolic signboard is fixed to the bottom stairpost outside the house. This is called a *chaleo*, and is made of bamboo bent into a small hoop on top, across which are stretched strands of red and white thread, so that it looks rather like a tennis racquet. (The dictionary gives *chaleo* as "a device shaped like Solomon's seal and made of strips of bamboo, serving as a sign that a thing is for sale, as a charm on a pot containing a potion, or as a boundary mark.") The *chaleo* acts as a warning to visitors not to gossip or speak any evil to the mother, or say anything as tactless as "My goodness, it's hot in here!" or "You poor thing, how can you bear it?" Such talk might weaken the mother's will and make her seven days' ordeal by fire that much harder.

The *yu fai* ceremony is conducted by an expert layman or laywoman, who first blesses the fire in the stove. He or she then chews a mixture of rice and salt, which has already been blessed by monks, and spits it out three times onto the mother's bare stomach as a protection against the fire, then again three times onto the stove itself. Holy water is also sprinkled on the stove, and a tray with the usual offerings of food, flowers, joss-sticks, and a candle is offered to the Spirit of Fire.

The mother now climbs onto another bed, on which she lies sideways. The midwife who delivered her baby stands on her, helping her body back to its normal shape. The mother goes over to the stove and *wai*'s to it, then climbs onto the banana-trunk bed again. The *yu fai* expert now blesses a yellow paste made from turmeric and a red one made from betel and spreads them over the mother's skin as moisturisers. This is repeated every day during the *yu fai* treatment.

Women who find the heat excessive are allowed to stop after three days and nights, but the correct time is at least seven continuous days. During this time visitors bring gifts of turmeric, dried fish, and bananas. The mother may also eat rice and salt and, after a few days, she is given *kaeng liang*, a thick soup made with *kapi*, or shrimp paste, to aid lactation.

The *yu fai* procedure sounds uncomfortably hot, but Thai women have undergone it for centuries, in their hundreds of thousands. It must surely have beneficial effects, or else why has it persisted for so long, as I believe it still does in some rural areas?

Another custom related to that of *yu fai* is designed to protect the baby itself during the first seven days of its life. Superstition has it that every new-born child is accompanied by its own *mae-sue*. The dictionary translates this as "a child's guardian angel," but according to my usual sources it is not necessarily a benevolent spirit at all; the *mae-sue* is simply a spirit which comes with the child. It may play with him, make him laugh, rock him to and fro (the Thai equivalent of "rock-a-bye baby on the tree-top" perhaps?), and guard him; or it may make him cry and do him harm. Westerners believe that when a tiny baby looks as if it is smiling, winking, or screwing up its face in various other weird ways, it is because the child needs to bring up wind; but the rural Thai belief is that the child is playing with its *mae-sue*.

The new-born baby must be protected from the spirit's playful, wayward, and unpredictable behavior. For this purpose, a piece of white cloth is hung above the head or side of the child's cradle. The cloth is roughly the size of an average magazine page, and has drawings on both sides. The drawing on the side facing away from the child represents the child's *mae-sue*. The spirit has different forms depending on the day of the week on which the child was born, and the drawing on the cloth must be made accordingly. The body is always that of a woman (*mae* means "mother"), but the head is that of a different beast for every day. The color of the skin varies from day to day – red for Sunday, cream or yellow for Monday, pink for Tuesday, and so on. (See Chapter 8 for "Colors of the Day").

The drawing on the side of the cloth facing inward towards the baby is always that of the king of the giants, Thao Wetsuwan. He wears a gold costume, and has a green skin. All other giants and spirits go in fear of Thao Wetsuwan, and this gives him the power to protect humans from them. Anyone who is afraid of giants and spirits often hangs up Thao Wetsuwan's picture on the wall. His presence on the piece of cloth hanging over the new-born baby's cradle protects the child from its own *mae-sue*.

Thao Wetsuwan is a well-known personality in Thai mythology. Huge statues of him form the two vertical pillars of a large gateway at Wat Pho, the Temple of the Reclining Buddha. Thao Wetsuwan was originally a human, who made daily merit by offering food to monks. One day he accidentally spilt some very hot sugar-cane juice on a monk's foot, causing the latter great pain. But instead of trying to help the monk. Thao Wetsuwan just stood there and laughed heartlessly. Because of this unkind act, Thao Wetsuwan was reborn in the world of giants, where he became king. But he suffered, and still continues to suffer, the consequences of his unkind behavior: He has permanently hot feet! Every day, other giants must come and bathe Thao Wetsuwan's feet to try and cool them, but it is no use; they remain as hot as ever – just as hot, in fact, as was the monk's foot when Thao Wetsuwan spilt the hot sugar-cane juice on it.

## When Traditions Intermingle

I once attended the opening ceremony of a large, new, plush Chinese restaurant in Bangkok. It was quite an eye-opening experience for me, and gave me some new insights into the subtle and harmonious blending of Thai and Chinese customs in Thailand.

The ceremony was due to begin at ten a.m., the invitation card said. The card was printed in English, Thai, and Chinese. Although the English text of the invitation did not say so, I knew that the ceremony was to be conducted by the Supreme Patriarch, the head of all Thailand's Buddhist monks. I had also been told that the Chinese text asked guests not to bring the usual gifts which Chinese folk everywhere always take to such ceremonies – baskets of flowers, gift vouchers and the like – but instead, to use whatever money they would have spent on such gifts as donations to the Po Tek Tung Foundation or the Kwong Sui (Cantonese) Association, both of them charity organizations.

Arriving at the restaurant at about 9.40 a.m., I was greeted by the restaurant manager. A steady stream of guests was arriving, practically all of them prosperous-looking local Chinese businessmen with a sprinkling of women. In spite of what the invitation card said, I was surprised to see that many of them were indeed bringing beautiful baskets of flowers. I asked the manager, in a whisper, why they were disregarding the request on the invitation card to give their money to charity instead.

"Ah," he said, "you must understand, we only printed that request in Chinese. To have printed it in Thai or English would have been most impolite."

. . . But the people bringing flowers were Chinese, surely? They certainly looked Chinese.

"Yes, they are Chinese. But remember, they are Thai-Chinese, and the ones bringing the flowers probably can't read Chinese – only Thai."

Pause for reflection . . . Does that tell us Westerners something maybe we had not thought about before? It certainly did in my case. . . .

Shortly afterwards I was delighted to see something I have never seen before, except in newspaper pictures: A Chinese lion dance (sometimes known as a dragon dance). This was performed just outside the restaurant by a group of five or six youths who from their features and dark complexions were very obviously not Chinese at all but pure Thai, and most probably country lads at that. One of them set up a stand with a large drum which he proceeded to beat fiercely, rhythmically, and deafeningly. The leader of the troupe donned a huge, ornate Chinese lion's head, and a younger boy put on a comic bald-headed mask. They swayed back and forth in a kind of short procession for a few minutes, working their way towards the restaurant entrance, and then came inside.

"Is this official or unofficial?" I asked the manager. "Unofficial," he answered, rather morosely I thought, "but we have to pay them just the same."

Once inside the doorway, the troupe immediately formed a three-boy-high column, stretching nearly fifteen feet up to the lofty ceiling. The top boy was only a little fellow of twelve or so, and at one stage he nearly fell off. But the others heard his yell for help in time, and quickly and gently let him down to the ground.

The troupe formed into procession again, with the lion's head prostrating itself and bowing at the manager's feet. The manager fed several 100-baht notes into the lion's mouth, which were quickly seized from inside. Meanwhile, the boy in the bald-headed mask was clawing at one of the manager's legs, and he too received a few more 100-baht notes.

Shortly after ten a.m. a limousine drove up, out of which stepped His Holiness the Supreme Patriarch, followed by eight monks, who emerged from a hired microbus. They took their places on a raised platform specially set up against the far wall of the restaurant, with the Supreme Patriarch on the extreme left. Most of the guests took their seats in the rows of chairs provided, although many remained at the back, chatting. The whole thing was somehow both very formal and very informal at the same time. It was hard to say which was louder, the Pali chanting of the monks, or the buzz of conversation from the five hundred or so guests.

The chanting continued for half an hour or so, with the monks holding the white cord called *sai sin*. Then the monks were given food, the restaurant thereby making merit. All the monks except the Supreme Patriarch sat round a table; he alone remained seated cross-legged on the platform, where food was brought to him.

After their meal was over (it was their last meal of the day, for no monk may eat after midday), the monks went back to the platform, and there was a further short spell of chanting. Then the restaurant management and close friends knelt before His Holiness, who blessed everyone by sprinkling holy water over them vigorously with a bunch of what looked like wooden sticks, resembling a short broom. The ceremony ended with His Holiness anointing both the large main doors with a pyramid of dots by dipping his finger in a special white paste, after which he applied small squares of gold leaf and then sprinkled the doors with holy water. As the limousine and microbus moved off, the lion-boys suddenly reappeared from nowhere, and His Holiness left amid the deafening rhythm of the drum.

After that there was a splendid spread of Chinese roast meats, spring rolls and other delicacies upstairs, and a good (and very filling) time was had by all.

## Some Like It Hot!

Thai food can be very, very spicy-hot. I will never forget the first time I bit accidentally and heavily on a chili. (It was my own fault. I had been in Thailand nearly a year and ought to have known better. But the conversation at my boss's farewell party was so lively that somehow my usual gastronomic vigilance slipped.) I nearly shot through the ceiling with the pain – my tongue, the roof of my mouth, and my throat were ablaze, and even after several glasses of iced water the agony persisted. I could eat nothing more that evening. I could not even talk (how nice for the other guests!) and limped home to two aspirins and an early bed.

You will gather that I am definitely not one of those fortunate Westerners who can enjoy Thai food at its hottest and spiciest.

On another occasion I had gone to Don Muang airport to meet the Chulalongkorn University professor in whose department I was working, who was returning from a trip overseas. I was with the professor's wife and another woman lecturer. We were early, and were sitting with glasses of orange juice on the second-floor open-air restaurant terrace.

I should perhaps mention that Thai eating habits are different from Western ones because there is less of a tendency towards fixed meal times. Instead "a little and often" seems to be more or less the rule; and so it was with the professor's wife. It was 5.30 p.m. and she had ordered a huge and delicious-looking plate of *lap*, a dish of minced beef originally from Northeast Thailand. "Like to try some?" she asked me. I took a forkful . . . OUCH! I made a wild grab for the other woman's orange juice (my own was finished), with which I managed to put out the fire. Afterwards I apologized for my rudeness, but the two women were shaking with laughter.

I might add that I am slowly improving. I can now eat a whole plate of *lap* and thoroughly enjoy it – provided I have got several glasses of water handy.

What can be said about the basic features of Thai cuisine? It is difficult to generalize about such a wide subject – perhaps even more so than with the cuisines of other countries. Thai food has traditionally taken over some of the best dishes from others lands. Indian, Chinese, Malaysian, and even Portuguese dishes were adopted centuries ago into this country, and adapted to suit Thai tastes and palates.

Examples of Portuguese origin are *foi thong* and *thong yip*, two delicious yellow sweetmeats which are rather similar to Middle-Eastern halva. Both of these have long been regarded as 100 percent Thai dishes. The many excellent varieties of Thai curry probably originated in India. Chinese influence on Thai eating habits may well have first been introduced via Chinese merchantmen, and later by the thousands of Chinese immigrants to this country.

Today, throughout the length and breadth of Thailand, it is virtually impossible to draw a hard and fast line between Thai and Chinese food; there is a continuous spectrum ranging from pure Thai at one end to pure Chinese at the other. Examples of "pure Thai" are *nam phrik pla thu*, mackerel with a spicy sauce (for details of the latter, see below), and a whole range of *tom yam*, or spicy sour soups made with lemongrass, kaffir lime leaf, and other standard ingredients, and containing almost any kind of seafood or meat you want. At the opposite end of the spectrum are such purely Chinese dishes as dim sum or small savoury dumplings, and, of course, Peking duck.

To those people who have sensitive palates and throats as I do, it may be of interest to know that in this country extremely spicy-hot foods are non-Chinese, but the converse is not always true: Mild dishes are not necessarily Chinese; some Thai dishes are also mild.

The Thai people themselves vary enormously in their tastes for spicy versus non-spicy food. This depends partly on which region of Thailand one is considering. Many natives of Bangkok have never even heard of some of the commonest dishes in the South, North, and Northeast, let alone tasted them. Food in North and Northeast Thailand tends to be very spicy indeed. Beware those little tell-tale specks of red chili, all you weak-tongued Westerners: Red for danger!

Another regional variation concerns that commonest of all Thai foods: Rice. People in the Central Plains and the South mostly eat ordinary rice, while in the Northeast and

North, sticky rice is normally eaten as the main dish. In Bangkok sticky rice (*khao nieo*) is regarded mainly as a dessert, to be eaten with mangoes when they are in season, plus coconut cream, or with other sweetmeats such as *sangkhaya*, a kind of coconut custard. People in the North and Northeast, on the other hand, often complain that ordinary rice eaten as the main dish leaves you hungry again after an hour or so; they refer to its as *mai yu thong* ("it doesn't stay in the stomach"). Central Plains people retort that sticky rice makes you sleepy . . . (And lazy?)

*Nam phrik*, the spicy sauce referred to above, is very popular as a "dip" all over Thailand. This takes different forms indifferent parts of the country. In the Bangkok area, *namprik* usually contains *kapi*, or shrimp paste, but not in other parts of Thailand. Whatever its form, *namprik* is usually eaten with large quantities of fresh vegetables, mostly raw. According to a Thai friend of mine, this is probably a major factor contributing to the overall level of good health in this country.

Within the last hundred years foreign influence has again been felt in Thai food. A good example is the dish known as *sa-tu*, which owes both its name and its style to that good old Western favorite, stew. But here again Thailand has subtly modified the dish to suit its own tastes. *Sa-tu* is usually made with chicken or ox-tongue.

Talking of *sa-tu* reminds me of another staple dish with a similar name in the West – *sa-khu*, or sago. (The English word comes from the Malay *sagu*, and I expect the Thai word does, too.) Westerners in Thailand who break into a large yawn at the thought of that dullest of desserts, sago pudding, must surely have been delighted, as I have often been, by the various Thai desserts based on *sa-khu piak* or "sticky sago," made with the gorgeous, delicate-flavored *lamyai* fruit from the North, or with pale mauve yam roots, black sticky rice, or shredded coconut.

There are many other varieties of Thai food which Westerners can enjoy without torturing their tongues – far, far too many to describe here. If you're lucky enough to have a good cook and haven't yet encouraged her to strike out on her own with some non-spicy Thai food of her own choosing, you don't know what you are missing.

To round off the meal, here are three favorite Thai sweetmeats (I nearly wrote "sweethearts") of mine. *Khao tom phat*, or "fried boiled rice" doesn't resemble rice at all, but is something like a very miniature and sticky, roly-poly, currant pudding in which the "currants" are black beans and which has a slice of pink banana running down the centre. *Kluai kuan* is banana boiled and stirred until it has the consistency of jam and is rich, sweet dark brown, sticky and gooey like its name. And *thong muan*, or "rolled gold," is a little nibbing sweetmeat which can't always make up its mind whether it is sweet or savory, because it sometimes contains *phak chi*, or local parsley. But it's delicious!

# CHAPTER FIVE
# Beliefs and Superstitions

## The Spirit in the Banyan Tree

I have already mentioned that Thai people worship a great many deities, and that this in no way conflicts with their profound Buddhist faith. In the section on "Calling Blessings on a New House" in Chapter 3, I referred briefly to the guardian spirit of a piece of land, who must be propitiated before laying the foundation stone of a new building. This spirit is known in Thai as *chao thi*, or "the Lord of the Place." Another name, especially if the spirit inhabits a large tree on or next to the site, is *thepharak*. There is a huge banyan tree at the back of our house, and my wife and her relatives who live with us believe that the *thepharak* which lives in this tree is the spirit who guards all of us living within the compound. It is generally believed that most spirits living in big trees are good ones.

My wife sometimes makes offerings to the spirit in the banyan tree. They are of the usual type: A flower, a candle, and a single joss-stick, which she lights while kneeling at the foot of the tree, plus a plate with three miniature soy sauce–type dishes containing boiled rice, a sweetmeat, and water, respectively.

My wife says that in the old days, if anyone wanted to cut down any big tree, it was considered important to ask permission beforehand from the spirit living in the tree. This was done by means of a similar ceremony with a candle and joss-sticks, and also an axe or long-handled hammer. The axe or hammer was placed leaning against the tree trunk. After two days, if it was still in the same position, this meant that the spirit had granted permission to cut the tree down; but if the axe or hammer had fallen down on the ground, the spirit did not agree, so the tree was left untouched.

And now, back to our own banyan tree.

One day when I came home from work I saw an unfamiliar and rather decorative object sitting in a small soup-dish on the dining-room table. When I asked what it was, I was told that it was a *bai si pak cham*, literally a *bai si* in the mouth of a dish. I have referred to the *bai si* in Chapter 3 when describing the preordination ceremony of a monk. The dictionary simply calls it "cooked rice topped with a boiled egg, used as an offering." *Bai si* can be of various shapes and sizes, depending on their function. This little one on our table was most attractive, with bright crimson flowers, shiny green banana leaves, and little cakes of various colors wedged in between.

A great deal of delicate skill had obviously gone into its making – the careful folding of the banana leaves, held together with *mai-klat*, sharp wooden pins cut from the stem of a coconut-palm leaf; and the "everlasting" flowers carefully picked from the garden. (The Thai name for this crimson flower is *ban mai ru roi* – "the blossom which doesn't know how to fade" – which the dictionary gives as "glove amaranth, *Gomphrena globosa*," botanists please note.)

I stared at the unfamiliar object. "What on earth's that?" I asked. So my wife told me the whole story.

Apparently it had been made by Mook, her sister's younger daughter, who was then nearly fifteen. Mook had made it as an offering which she had vowed or promised to give to the spirit in the banyan tree at the back of our house. The reason for Mook's promise was simple: Her mother had told Mook she might give her a small sum of money as a New Year present, if she had enough spare cash; and Mook had prayed to the spirit in tree that this would happen. In her prayer, Mook promised the spirit an offering of a *bai si pak cham* if her wish were granted. And it was granted!

I feel it is worth repeating what I have said earlier: This ritual of begging a favor from a spirit, and promising to reward the spirit if the wish is granted, is pretty well universal in Thailand; it is the Thai way. Men and women beg for all sorts of things from many different spirits, such as certain especially revered Buddha statues, images of gods, goddesses, former national heroes and heroines, and so on. An infertile couple may beg for a child; a sick person, for a cure; and it may come as no surprise to learn that many people beg for a winning lottery ticket! In all cases the procedure is the same: A promise of some specific offering is made provided the wish is granted; if and when the wish is granted, the promise is honored – *always*.

## Curing a Sick Child

In describing the topknot-cutting ceremony in Chapter 3, I mentioned that topknots (*chuk* in Thai) have been grown on young children's heads for generations, and are still grown, mainly as a cure for persistent sickliness, feverishness, or a tendency towards accidents during babyhood.

Besides the topknot there are other ways of curing a chronically sick or accident-prone child. The most obvious one which comes to mind is – why not consult a doctor? But the answer in Thailand is the same as it always has been: The dire shortage of rural doctors. His Majesty the King's ceaseless effort to bring free medical service to those living in remote areas is giving valuable help where it is most needed. But in such a large country where perhaps nearly 30 million people live far away from towns, the development of this service is necessarily a slow process. And parents such as farmers in other rural areas can ill afford the recurring expense of private doctor's fees. Even the traditional herbal medicine practitioner cannot reach all the remote families to whom be could be of help.

Perhaps the commonest way of dealing with a sickly infant is to consult the abbot or some other respected monk at the local temple. The monk may again suggest growing a topknot, or he may recommend some form of "adoption" of the child. This kind of "adoption" is in spirit only; the child continues living at home with its parents.

There are three main kinds of "adoption." The monk may suggest asking a *luang pho,* or Buddha statue, to adopt the child and take care of it. This will make the child healthy again. The Buddha statue may be the one in the local temple, or perhaps a more famous one somewhere else. There are hundreds of specially revered Buddha statues in temples throughout the land. One of the most famous is Luang Pho Sothon at Wat Sothon in Chachoengsao, about 35 miles east of Bangkok, which I have described in the previous chapter. This statue has a tremendous reputation for curing the sick.

The second type of "adoption" is that in which a *chao pho* or *chao mae* – the image of a god or goddess – is asked to protect the child. These are also revered images, but of deities or spirits, not of the Lord Buddha. There are a great many of these in shrines up and down the country. One deity which I have already described is the Lord Brahma and his much-visited shrine in the Grand Hyatt Erawan Hotel compound. Another type of deity which may also be asked to "adopt" a sickly child is the *Chao Pho* Lak Mueang or guardian spirit of a city, which inhabits the city pillar. Near the seaside resort of Bang Saen on the east coast of the Gulf of Thailand there is the shrine of *Chao Mae* Sammuk, the spirit of a local girl who threw herself over a cliff because of a broken heart. She is much revered by the people of that district, and just as with any spirit held in high esteem locally, she is sometimes asked to "adopt" a sickly child because she is believed to have the power to cure it. (Her legend is in the next chapter.)

The third method of "adoption" is to ask some living person of good character to protect and "adopt" the child – someone looked up to by both the child's parents, such as a monk or the abbot at the local temple, or perhaps a grandmother or other elderly relative of the child.

In all three types of "adoption" the procedure is virtually the same. Loops of the sacred white *sai sin* thread are tied round the child's wrists, and the sickly infant is then presented without any special ceremony. Respectfully the parents beg the Buddha statue, the spirit or deity, or the living person, as the case may be, to "adopt" the child and protect it from further sickness and harm.

Sure enough, the child is invariably cured. The only snag with "adoption" by a Buddha statue or the image of a spirit or deity is that the parents must remember never to slap the child when it has been naughty. If they do, the child will immediately become ill again, though it may recover after a day or two. (This sounds like a wonderful opportunity for shrewd tiny tots to indulge in a bit of mild blackmail and get away with it!)

When I was writing this, a friend told me that she had the white *sai sin* thread tied round her wrists as part of her "Freshy" initiation ceremony at Chiang Mai University. I believe this act also symbolizes the idea of protection from evil influences by the student body.

## The Friendly Little *Jing-jok*

On my very first night in Thailand, in October 1965, I went for a stroll with another new arrival. We walked down Sukhumvit Soi 4 (Soi Nana Tai), at that time much more of a country lane than it is now. Suddenly our eyes were attracted by a new and interesting sight: A private house had one of those ornamental, mock old-fashioned lanterns by the gate, a product of Western culture, with a single electric light bulb inside; and there, silhouetted in black on the inside of the frosted glass of the "lantern," was a rather decorative reptilian shape. "If only I'd brought my camera!" we both exclaimed simultaneously.

It was, of course, one of those well known Thai creatures, a *jing-jok*. (The word is usually written *ching-chok* in Romanized spelling, but in this book I shall spell it with two "J's," which approximates more nearly the actual Thai sound as well as the Thai spelling.) It was the first *jing-jok* either of us had seen, even though it was only a silhouetted shape standing out boldly against the luminous yellow pane of the mock lantern. I wish I could have just one baht for every *jing-jok* I have seen in the years since then!

of the mock lantern. I wish I could have just one baht for every *jing-jok* I have seen in the years since then!

Other Westerners' first encounters with this harmless little creature may not always have been so pleasant. I remember once some acquaintances from Scotland arrived in Bangkok very tired; they had had no sleep for two whole nights. They had four young children with them, including a three-month-old baby. They were shown into their apartment by the Thai friend who had chosen it for them. As soon as they opened the living-room door, the Scottish lady let out a loud shriek. Something squiggly and squirmy had dropped from the wall onto the floor at her feet. Dazed and weary from lack of sleep, the poor woman felt sure it was some particularly repulsive and giant tropical insect. But of course it was not – it was only a harmless little *jing-jok*.

If anyone reading this has just arrived in Thailand on their first trip and has not yet met one of these creatures, maybe I should explain that they are a species of house-lizard. About two or three inches long, they look something like tiny crocodiles. Their hands and feet (I am no biologist – if hands and feet are not the correct terms, I hope the experts will excuse me) look almost human with their tiny little fingers, and once you have seen these you will realise they are not insects but reptiles. They are sometimes known as "geckos," but this word also applies to a rather larger creature called the *tookae*, which is also fairly common in this country, and which I will deal with briefly at the end of this section.

The *Oxford Dictionary* defines "gecko" simply as "a house lizard found in warm climates," while the *Encyclopedia Britannica* has this to say: "The names 'gecko,' 'tokay,' and 'cheechak' (*sic*) are based on the calls of various species of gecko . . . All species are insectivorous." I suspect that the Thai word *jing-jok* may have been adapted from the

Readers who, like me, prefer a passive to an active existence during leisure hours may have spent as many hours as I have done lying on the sofa studying the *jing-jok*'s social life on the walls and ceiling. This seems to consist mainly of staying transfixed to one spot as though fast asleep, punctuated by sudden wild dashes across the wall (or ceiling) at incredible speeds in pursuit of their lady-love. Occasionally, too, an apparently sleeping *jing-jok* will dart its little head forward and back again in a quick knife-like action which betrays its insectivorous nature – its staple diet consists of careless mosquitoes which don't watch where they're going.

You may also have heard the *jing-jok*'s little chattering cry, which sounds very much like a human tongue clicking when we go "Tch! Tch!" to warn someone – or to tell them off! This similarity in sound has given rise to a very natural old Thai superstition. If you hear that "Tch! Tch!" cry just as you're about to leave the house – then don't! In fact, says the superstition, if you hear the *jing-jok*'s cry just as you're about to do anything at all – don't do it! I don't know how many Thais still take this warning or portent seriously, but like most superstitions, elderly rural folk still believe in it.

Another superstition says the *jing-jok* can bring you good luck. Here is an example of how this actually happened. The mother of a Thai friend of ours was going out to buy a lottery ticket. She asked her daughter what number she should buy. Just at that moment the daughter heard the cry of a *jing-jok* nearby. The daughter quickly thought, *jing-jok*; JJ; jet-jet. "Jet is the Thai for "seven," so she told her mother to buy a ticket ending in 77. Sure enough, the ticket won two hundred baht! Not very much, you may say, but then, the *jing-jok* is not a very large creature, is it? What else can you expect from a mere two inches of reptile?

Well, in fact, you can expect quite a lot of information, according to my wife's book on portents and omens. The message the *jing-jok* brings will depend on which direction its "Tch! Tch!" cry comes from. If the cry comes from behind you, this signifies trouble from someone who is jealous of you – so watch out! If it comes from your left, this means your efforts during the next few days will be successful, and you will win respect and deference from everyone – yes, sir or madam! But if the cry comes from the right side, you may expect some form of suffering. Best of all is a *jing-jok* crawling over your foot. It may tickle, but it will bring you great success!

My wife adds the following: if you see a *jing-jok* with a double or forked tail, which is very rare, this is especially lucky; while if you are sitting down and a *jing-jok* drops onto the floor in front of you either dead or dying, this again means bad luck. Here's hoping it does not happen to you!

Now a brief word about the *tukae*. This belongs to the same family as the *jing-jok*, but is much larger – up to ten inches or even afoot long. They are not seen as much as they used to be, but their loud cry is often heard just outside the house. First there is a crescendo of quick, short grunts, for all the world as if the creature was winding itself up, then out comes the first cry of "tu-kae!" It sounds rather like a sort of super-cuckoo. If you hear seven or more cries of "tu-kae!" in quick succession, this will bring you good luck. So, once you hear the first cry of the *tukae*, count the ones that follow very carefully!

# Believe It or Not . . .

Here is a mixed bag of Thai superstitions and sayings.

## Never on a Wednesday

When should you have your hair cut?

If you have it cut on a Sunday, this will bring you long life. On a Monday, it will bring you health and happiness; and on a Tuesday, power.

Wednesday? Never, never have your hair cut on a Wednesday, say the Thais. The results will be nothing short of disastrous. Have you noticed that many barber's shops in Thailand, especially upcountry, are closed on Wednesdays? That is the reason.

A haircut on a Thursday means the *thevada*, or guardian angels, will protect you; on a Friday, you will never go in want; and on a Saturday, you will gain admiration.

But Saturdays are not good days for other things. Anything new is bad on a Saturday – especially moving into a new house, wearing new clothes, or using any new possession such as a car or even a refrigerator. (Owing to bad planning on my part, our new refrigerator was supposed to arrive on a Saturday, but luckily it was held up and didn't arrive until the following Tuesday.)

## Trees and Flowers

Thailand has many beliefs about trees, plants, and flowers. Some kinds of trees are unlucky if grown in one's garden or compound; others bring good luck.

Sometimes these beliefs have evolved from a similarity in the sounds of words, or from double meanings. Many Buddhist temples have frangipani or temple-trees growing in their grounds. These trees bear a beautiful and fragrant white

138

flower. Nevertheless, they should never be grown at home because their Thai name, *Lanthom*, sounds similar to *rathom*, which means "heartbroken."

The same reasoning applies to a kind of local fern called *prong*; it sounds like *plong*, meaning "to dispose of." This fern is, in fact, often used to decorate coffins.

*Champi* and *Champa* are two other trees in the same category; the first, whose Latin name is *Michelia longifolta*, suggests the expression *pracham pi*, or "yearly," and the belief is that if grown at home, it will bring illness to the family every year. The second (English name "champak") implies that you will lose all your money!

In the opposite category are trees and plants which are supposed to bring good luck if grown at home. Among these is the *canna*, a tall, graceful plant with yellow, orange, and pink flowers. This is often grown as a boundary hedge because its Thai name is *phuttharaksa*, or "the Buddha protects." Another lucky plant is the *mayom*, or Chinese gooseberry, which produces a pleasant-tasting fruit. It is lucky because its name sounds like *niyom*, meaning "popularity." A sprig of *mayom* is often used by monks at ceremonies to sprinkle holy water over people and buildings in order to bless them.

The belief about *mayom* is part of a more general one that all trees and plants whose name begins with *ma-* bring good luck if grown in one's garden. There are forty-nine such names listed in the dictionary, and the reason they are lucky is that they all produce edible fruit or leaves used in cooking.

I was once told that the short syllable *ma-* is derived from the word *mak* meaning "betel," the seed which used to be chewed throughout Thailand and which stained teeth red. (Nowadays this seems to have been largely replaced by chewing-gum!)

Some of the more common trees and plants beginning with *ma-* are: *makrut*, or kaffir lime, whose leaf, rather like a bay-leaf, is used in cooking; *makok*, the olive or hog-plum from which the once tiny riverside "village of olives" or "Bang makok" got its name, later shortened to "Bangkok"; *makhuea khao*, eggplant; *makhuea thet*, tomato; *manao*, lime; *ma-phrao*, coconut palm; *ma-phlap*, persimmon; *mamuang*, mango; *mamuang himaphan*, cashew-nut tree; *malako*, papaya; and *makham* or tamarind.

The *makham*'s branches are very tough and springy, and even the slenderest of them can take a person's weight without snapping. In Thai such a tree is called *niao* or "sticky," and for this reason it is believed that if you grow a tamarind tree in front of your house, your money will become "sticky" too – it will always stick with you!

Two other superstitions about flowers and trees have come my way. A red hibiscus should never be worn at a religious ceremony, because executioners used to wear such a flower above their ear during executions. And an *asok* tree (Latin name *Saraca indica*) is unlucky if grown at home, because its name, like that of the greenish color I mentioned earlier, sounds like the word *sok*, meaning "sadness."

## Animals

Thailand has its fair share of beliefs about animals. Black cats are generally considered unlucky, but apart from this the cat is regarded as a noble animal. It is allowed inside the house, and if a cat brings her litter of kittens into the house, this is very lucky. It is said that a cat will always make its owner rich, because it prays for wealth so the owner will buy it a gold dish to eat from!

Dogs, on the other hand, are usually considered debased creatures, not fit to be allowed in the house. Some people

Dogs, on the other hand, are usually considered debased creatures, not fit to be allowed in the house. Some people say dogs are only waiting for their owner to die so they can eat his bones!

Now for some other animals. Speak gently and politely to a vulture if it flies around your property, and call it *Chao Phya* Hong Thong, or "most noble golden swan," or it may bring you a fire, bankruptcy, or some other disaster. The same goes for a monitor lizard on your premises – you must show it proper respect by addressing it as a "golden dragon."

I mentioned in an earlier chapter that a screech-owl is the messenger of death; if one is heard flying over the house at night in a westerly direction, anyone in the house who is ill will surely die.

Now here is a belief about young children and evil spirits. If you look up the Thai word *nakliat* in the dictionary, you will find it means "loathsome, objectionable; (of a face) ugly; (of a child) lovely". Is that strange – or isn't it?

Not really. A bonny child is often deliberately and loudly spoken of as *nakliat*, so that the ever-present evil spirits waiting to pounce and steal the child away from its parents will hear it being called "ugly." That way, they will lose interest in it and go away in search of a prettier child somewhere else.

## Now for a Few Sayings about Women

Thai women walk softly, with extreme grace, and bolt-upright. They are taught as children not to stamp their feet, because that would be an insult to *Mae Phra* Thorani, or Mother Earth (the spirit I mentioned earlier, in connection with not standing on the raised thresholds of doorways). A young woman who walks heavily and noisily is scolded with the remark: "There you go again, clomp-clomp! One day marries, her husband's mother will take a dislike to her, and this will cause her own parents to lose face. Another saying has it that if you walk with a heavy tread, your money will fly away from you – and no one wants that to happen. These sayings are all designed to make young girls walk gracefully.

An unmarried woman should never sing in the kitchen, or she will end up with an old man for a husband. When she is pounding chilies with a mortar, if the mortar does not make a loud noise, the saying goes that no man will ever marry her; it means she is not *kha-yan*, not hardworking, and a rotten cook into the bargain!

As those who have been in Thailand during the rainy season may know, the rain may be pouring down in buckets in one part of Bangkok, while a mile away it is bone-dry and stays that way. Thais call this *fon tok mai thao fa*: "It isn't raining all over the sky." A very neat way of putting it. And this saying is also used rather subtly in a different context. If a rich man is distributing gifts or largesse to all and sundry, perhaps to celebrate some special occasion such as the New Year or his birthday, and he happens to miss someone out, the unfortunate non-recipient will go up to the rich benefactor and instead of putting it baldly by asking "What about me?" he will simply say "It isn't raining all over the sky!"

Do you remember the old joke about the office-boy who asked for the day off to go to his grandmother's funeral and was later discovered watching a football match? Thailand has its own counterpart for that story, but the joke in this case depends on a play on words.

A young army officer asked his superior for three days' leave of absence to attend his grandmother's cremation ceremony. Just as Westerners might say "I'm going to bury my grandmother," so Thais sometimes say "I'm going to burn my grandmother," and that was how the young officer put it. Three weeks later he made the same request again. "But you did that three weeks ago!" exclaimed his superior officer. At this stage I must interrupt the story to explain that the spoken Thai word for "grandmother" sounds exactly the same as that for "grass." The young officer replied: "Oh, but that time I only stayed at home to burn grass. This time I really am going to burn my grandmother!"

# CHAPTER SIX

# Legends

## The *Ramakian*

One of the first delights to which foreign arrivals to Thailand are treated is usually a display of Thai classical dancing. The chances are that what is shown in the dance is an episode, or part of an episode, from the great Thai epic story, the *Ramakian*.

Various Western authors have written books of great scholarship about the *Ramakian*. It has been aptly and accurately called "the sheet-anchor of a main facet of Thai culture," and "the most important theme in the field of the Thai arts."

The story of the *Ramakian* was adapted by the Thais, perhaps before the thirteenth century A.D., from the great Indian epic story, the *Ramayana* ("The Life of Rama"), which, says the *Encyclopedia Britannica*, was written about twenty-three hundred years ago by the poet Valmiki. The story describes the royal birth of Rama in the kingdom of Ayodhya (from which came the name of Ayutthaya, Thailand's former capital city); Rama's marriage to King Janaka's daughter, Sita (changed to "Sida" in the Thai version); Sita's abduction by the demon king Ravana ("Thotsakan" in the *Ramakian* – the name means "ten heads"), who carries her off to Longka (the present-day Sri Lanka); Rama's long struggle against Ravana to rescue Sita; Ravana's ultimate defeat by Rama, and Rama's return to claim his throne.

The *Ramayana* story, always popular in India, has spread iIn various forms throughout Southeast Asia. According to one Western writer the version of the Thai form, the *Ramakian*, written in 1785 by King Rama I, the first King of the present Royal House of Chakri, is the most widely read in Thailand. The original story has been adhered to as far as the main events are concerned; gods, demons, angels, humans, animals (especially monkeys), and giants take part in the great battle between Rama and Thotsakan in the forests and cities of a legendary Thailand of long ago. But in its adaptation to Thai cultural ways the story has taken on subtle changes and has become somehow softened, giving it its essential "Thai-ness."

A typically Thai feature is that besides the classical love theme between Rama and Sida, the feeling of love and warmth between a mother and child is also introduced. This is one of the themes in the *Ramakian* which teachers always impress on their pupils.

The Western writer mentioned above suggests that the wise King Rama I, while adapting the *Ramayana* story to Thai cultural values, found in it away of providing continuity with the ancient Thai culture, which was endangered by the fall of Ayutthaya In 1767. The writer says he has been much impressed by the variety of ways in which the *Ramakian* story influences the Thai people. He says one may see families walking slowly through the galleries of the Emerald Buddha Temple on Sunday afternoons, looking at the great murals depicting the story, while parents tell the story to their children. He adds that city, street, and even personal names are drawn from the *Ramakian*.

Indeed, there can surely be few, if any, folk tales anywhere in the world which permeate such a wide range of national culture and everyday life as does the *Ramakian* in Thailand. If one were to take all the fairy tales of the brothers Grimm and of Hans Christian Andersen, the Arabian Nights and the fables of Aesop and Lafontaine, and put them all together, even then one would probably not begin to equal the length as well as the universality of general knowledge of the *Ramakian* in this country.

Episodes carefully chosen by the Ministry of Education are compulsory reading in *Prathom* (primary) and in *Mathayom* (secondary) schools throughout the land. To be strictly accurate, King Rama I's version was written in traditional Thai epic verse form; part of this version was adapted and rewritten in a different classical verse form by his son King Rama II, and it is this later version which is studied in the schools.

In the sphere of classical stage drama, the Ramakian stories are the subjects of the two main Thai drama forms: The *khon*, or masked play, in which the actors and actresses do not speak, their lines being chanted by singers in the orchestra, and the *lakhon*, or musical play, in which the players themselves recite lines.

As already mentioned, Thai classical dancing also draws largely for its subject-matter on the *Ramakian*, and so does the *nang yai*, or shadow-play. In addition to this wealth of cultural material, murals and bas-reliefs in countryside and city temples (the finest bas-reliefs are those at the Temple of the Reclining Buddha), rural paintings, cottage handicraft industries, temple rubbings, of which quite cheap but lovely copies can be bought all over Bangkok, as can exquisite tooled-leather traceries used in the shadow-plays, wood carvings, simplified folk tales, music, songs: All of these (and

147

probably more) draw their inspiration from the *Ramakian*.

The *Ramakian* falls into three main sections, comprising in all 138 episodes. The second section, which is the most popular, deals with Thotsakan's abduction of Sida, and Rama's recovery of her. This forms the theme of the bas-reliefs at the Temple of the Reclining Buddha, and also of the episodes most commonly studied in schools and performed on the stage.

In the following section I shall tell the story of one of those episodes.

An episode from the *Ramakian*:

### "The Floating Lady"

No! It's not Ophelia. It is probably fair to say that the Thai story of "The Floating Lady" is far better known, by more adults and children among the general public, than even "Hamlet" is in the West. The story of the "Floating Lady" is one of the best known of the 138 episodes of the classical Thai epic story, the *Ramakian*.

The story of "The Floating Lady," known in Thai as *"Nang Loi,"* as it is related below, adheres fairly closely to the version in the school text-book used in *Mathayom Suksa* 4 – the fourth year of secondary school in Thailand. In this version, part of the story is told in classical Thai verse form as composed by King Rama II in the Second Reign of the present Chakri Dynasty.

When the story begins, the war between Rama, the handsome king, and Thotsakan, the ten-headed demon king of Longka (supposed to be the island kingdom known today as Sri Lanka), had already been going on for a very long time. The reason for the war was Thotsakan's abduction of Sida, Rama's exquisitely beautiful queen, and Rama's attempt to get her back.

Weary of the long war, Thotsakan sought a way of bring-ing it to an end – in his favor, of course. He knew that if Rama could be somehow convinced that his lovely wife Sida was dead, he would call a halt to the fighting, because there would be no point in going on with it. Thotsakan therefore thought up a really fiendish plan to do this.

He summoned his niece, Benchakai, who had learnt magic from her father, Phiphek. Thotsakan ordered her to use her magic powers to disguise herself so that she looked exactly like Sida. She was then to arrange to be found, apparently dead, near the place where Rama's army of monkeys was encamped. Thotsakan promised Benchakai a reward if Rama was successfully taken in by this ruse, and as a result called off the war against Longka.

As soon as she heard her uncle's plan, Benchakai was ter-rified. She knew she would be put to death by Rama's sol-dier-monkeys if her trick was discovered; but she also knew just as surely that her uncle would punish her ruthlessly if she refused to do his bidding.

Weeping, Benchakai was taken to the park where Thotsakan held the beautiful Sida a prisoner. On the way Benchakai stopped to ask her mother, Trichada (so called because her hair was braided in a triple knot), what she ought to do. Her mother advised her to carry out Thotsakan's or-ders.

Arriving at the pavilion where Sida spent her long, lonely days, Benchakai threw herself at the queen's feet and told her that she, Benchakai, was completely at her uncle Thotsakan's mercy. (The reason for this was rather compli-cated and forms part of an earlier episode.) But her terror had made Benchakai cunning; even while she was sobbing her heart out to Sida, she was carefully studying and memo-rizing every detail of her appearance and behavior. By the time she took her leave of Sida, Benchakai had a complete image of the queen firmly fixed in her mind.

Benjakai retired to a solitary spot and used her magic to change herself into an exact likeness of Sida, after which she returned to her uncle. Thotsakan was completely taken in by Benchakai's disguise; he believed that the lovely Sida, whom he had desired for so long, had at last come to give herself to him, and flinging his arms round her he promised her half his kingdom.

When Benchakai at last managed to break free from his grasp, she quickly changed herself back to her own form. Thotsakan, at first enraged and frustrated by being thus cheated out of his heart's desire, soon had a change of mood. He realised that if he himself, the demon king, had been taken in by this clever disguise, how much more easily would Rama, who was a human, be deceived!

Early one morning shortly afterwards, Rama went down to the water's edge to bathe. As ever, his thoughts were of one subject only: His lost and beloved wife, Sida. He sang a love song softly to himself.

Suddenly Rama saw the body of a beautiful woman, apparently washed upon the shore as if it had been floating on the water. Approaching, he realised with growing horror that the body was that of Sida.

Beside himself with grief, he slowly sank to his knees and with the greatest tenderness raised the body from the ground.

Rama's supporters heard his loud weeping and came hurrying down to the shore, led by the valiant white monkey, Hanuman, Rama's trusted servant and a general in his army. Not for nothing was Hanuman singled out for high command, for he was extremely intelligent. It took him only a second or two to recover from the shock of seeing what appeared to be Sida's corpse, after which his sharp eyes picked out two suspicious-looking details.

Turning to the king, he said, "Do not weep, Sire. That is not Queen Sida. Just look at the direction of the current – it is flowing towards Longka. It could not possibly have washed that body up at this spot. Another thing, this corpse does not resemble a corpse at all; there are no signs of decay! Let us set fire to it, and see what happens."

So Hanuman ordered his soldiers to build a funeral pyre and place the corpse on it. Naturally, after only a few seconds the heat became too much for Benjakai; she changed abruptly back to her own form, and flew up into the air in an attempt to escape. But Hanuman had seen through her trickery, and was after her in a flash. Seizing her by her long hair, he dragged her down and back to the camp. Here Benjakai revealed the whole story of her uncle's plot. But Rama showed mercy on her, and sparing her life he sent her back to Longka to tell her uncle of his latest failure.

My everyday English prose simply cannot do justice to the effect King Rama II's epic verses have on Thai readers. No one other than a Thai can appreciate the poignancy of such passages as the description of Rama's grief on discovering what he takes to be Sida's body.

## *Chao Mae* Sammuk

Besides the *Ramakian*, Thailand certainly has its fair share of other legends and folk tales, perhaps even more than some other countries. Naturally many of them involve love and romance. Some of these old stories are based, if not demonstrably on truth, at least on real places; and one such place is the hill known as Khao Sammuk, just north of Bangkok's nearest seaside resort, Bang Saen.

A lovelorn lass named Sammuk gave her name to this hill, the north side of which falls away in a sheer cliff down to the sea. The lover's-leap spot from which she is supposed to have jumped to her death can be reached partly by car and partly on foot – that is, if you are reasonably sure-footed.

Bang Saen is well worth a day trip by car, but make it in mid-week, if you can; it is pretty crowded at weekends. It is on the way to Pattaya, just a few miles after you pass through the provincial town of Chonburi. A small road

leads off to the right, and this turns north when it meets the coast, becoming a two-mile stretch alongside the beach pleasantly fringed with massive pines and palms.

To reach Khao Sammuk, follow this beach road north-ward until it curves inland to the right. Soon you will see Khao Sammuk ahead and to the left, a small steepish hill dotted with semi-luxury villas facing south.

A side road forks left and takes you up to a vantage point, where there is a roofed-over observation seat like a rather elongated bus shelter. From here you get a delightful view to the south, looking across the way you have just come: The sweeping curve of Bang Saen Bay, the wide horizon of the sea, distant mountains and islands.

If one continues along the same road past the viewpoint, it becomes suddenly very countrified – nothing but trees and the sea below. It is almost like driving along a country lane in Devon in England in the springtime. After dipping sharply downward the road forks, the right-hand fork climb-ing again to where there is a small sort of cafe-cum-bar at a hairpin bend in the road. This has a pleasant terrace with tables and chairs high above the sea.

Going round to the back of the cafe-bar, one should be able to find the primitive footpath which leads up to the top of the rocky promontory beyond. Take care, and be sure to wear non-slip soles. After a short ten minute climb the path peters out onto a broad slab of rock fringed by bushes. One can sit on the rock and absorb another quite breathtaking view, northward this time: The wide curve of Chonburi Bay with Chonburi town glistening in the distance and a string of majestic mountains on the right.

It was from this same slab of rock that the unfortunate Sammuk is supposed to have plunged to her death. It is a typical country folk-tale: She was of humble birth, but fell in love with a young man from a rich family. His parents refused to let him marry her, and apparently it did not occur to the young couple to elope – or else it simply was not done. Instead, the poor girl threw herself over the cliff.

But, says the legend, instead of floating away out to sea as would have been expected, Sammuk's body somehow remained attached to the base of the cliff. The local people rescued the body and put it in a cave nearby. (I have no idea when all this was supposed to have happened; it was as usual with legends, simply "a long time ago"). The cave immediately and miraculously became filled with a large quantity of knives, forks, spoons, plates, dishes, and other utensils, all of pure gold.

When the people of the nearby villages, Bang Saen and Angsila, heard of all this miracle cutlery, they came to investigate and found they were able to borrow this opulent tableware and kitchenware without any apparent evil consequences. They formed the habit of doing this whenever they were holding a party or ceremony of any kind.

But human nature being what it is, some of the valuable gold objects were inevitably "lost" and were not returned to the cave. Sammuk's spirit (known in Thai as *Chao Mae* Sammuk – *Chao Mae* means a goddess or female spirit) naturally became very angry at this dishonesty. She showed her

displeasure in no uncertain manner by promptly abandon-
ing her cave and sealing up the entrance after her, which
effectively put a stop to the borrowing of the gold utensils.

Realizing they had deeply offended *Chao Mae* Sammuk,
the local people felt very remorseful. To appease the angry
spirit, they immediately built a shrine for her at the foot of
the cliff.

If one takes the coast road round the headland, one can
see the shrine, *San Chao Mae* Sammuk. It is regarded as symbolizing true love, and local people in need of help come to
the shrine to beg *Chao Mae* Sammuk's aid. They promise to
bring her a coconut if she grants their wish. I have heard
that local fishermen are strong believers in this spirit's power
and place firm reliance on her protection whenever they
set out to sea.

# The Buddha's Footprint*

In the past, as today, Thailand derived much moral strength
from its kings through their firm adherence to the teachings of the Lord Buddha. One such monarch was King
Songtham of the Ayutthaya Period, who reigned from 1610
to 1628 A.D. It was he who issued the command which
resulted in the discovery of the Buddha's Footprint, one of
Thailand's most sacred relics.

The story goes that during King Songtham's reign a group
of Thai monks went on a pilgrimage to Sri Lanka, the first
country outside India where Buddhism took root and flour-
ished after the Lord Buddha's death. Their purpose was to

*Most of the material is taken from a paper read to the Siam Society by
HRH Prince Bidyalankarana on December 20, 1934.

visit the Buddha's Footprint which they knew existed on one of the island's highest mountains, Adam's Peak.

The Sri Lankan monks, however, asked their Thai brethren, "Why have you come here? According to the Sacred Books, there is a Buddha's Footprint in your own country."

On their return to Thailand the monk-pilgrims reported this conversation to King Songtham. The King immediately ordered a nation wide search for the footprint.

It was in the year 1623 (according to one historian) that the Governor of Saraburi Province sent a dramatic message to the King. He said that a hunter named Bun had discovered a huge footprint on a rock near the foot of a hill known as Golden Hill. Bun had shot and wounded a deer, which ran away and disappeared in thick undergrowth. Shortly afterwards the deer reappeared, apparently completely unhurt.

The astonished Bun crawled under the thick scrub and found a hole in a rock filled with clear, pure water. He drank some, and was immediately and miraculously cured of a painful skin disease from which he had been suffering.

Bun slowly and painstakingly emptied all the water out of the hollow in the rock, and found it was shaped in the likeness of a huge footprint. Knowing the King's urgent desire to find the Buddha's Footprint, Bun immediately reported his discovery to the Governor of Saraburi.

When the King received the Governor's message, he was overjoyed. The miraculous healing powers of the footprint on the hill proved without doubt that this was the sacred Buddha's Footprint of which the Sri Lanka monks had spoken.

King Songtham at once set out in state from Ayutthaya to see the footprint for himself. He made the first part of the journey by river, landing at a spot now known as Tha Ruea or "boat landing." From there he continued overland, with the hunter Bun as guide.

The King's delight on seeing the footprint knew no bounds. He lit a great many candles and joss-sticks, and saluted the holy relic over and over again.

King Songtham dedicated to the footprint all the surrounding land within a ten mile radius. He ordered a big temple built on the site, as well as a twenty metre wide road covering the thirteen miles from Tha Ruea to Golden Hill. On the river itself a royal pavilion was built at a spot which was named Tha Chao Sanuk, or "the landing-stage of royal enjoyment."

After King Songtham's death, later kings of the Ayutthaya Period visited the footprint, some of them regularly each year. These visits took place after the rice harvest was over. Improvements and repairs were made to the Temple and grounds, and it became a royal pleasure-ground as well as a shrine. A book compiled during the reign of King Taksin of Thonburi just before the start of the present Chakri Dynasty describes the arrangements for a typical royal visit to the footprint by one of the last of Ayutthaya's kings.

A huge procession of barges bore the King and his large retinue, as well as the princes and their families; the journey up-river from Ayutthaya to Tha Ruea took a whole day. All along the river banks the people turned out to see the royal procession, and to make merit. At Tha Ruea a stay of at least two days was made, after which the fourteen mile journey overland began. The procession included 144 official elephants and sixty horses. Royalty traveled in carriages, while bullock-carts bore all the baggage, provisions and other necessities. (The carts and bullocks were requisitioned from houses in the surrounding countryside; any house which failed to provide a cart was fined one and a half baht).

The following day the King, his family and his personal retinue visited the temple. Inside, the King lit candles and joss-sticks, covered parts of the footprint with gold leaf, and presented it with gifts, particularly a pair of trees, one of gold and the other of silver. Outside the temple he scattered gold and silver flowers among his followers. Entertainments followed: Boxing, fencing, plays, and fireworks. Great quantities of food and gifts were offered to the monks. The festivities continued for a full week, after which the huge royal procession returned to Ayutthaya.

The Temple of the Footprint became more and more richly endowed and filled with treasures. But during the final sacking of Ayutthaya by the Burmese in 1767 all these riches were looted, and the temple was burnt to the ground.

King Rama I, Founder of the Chakri Dynasty, ordered the temple rebuilt and requested his younger brother, the Deputy King, to supervise its construction. The Deputy King went to Golden Hill with an army including artists, craftsmen and artisans. Being a devout man with a deep veneration for the footprint, he walked the entire fourteen miles from Tha Ruea, carrying on his shoulder a piece of timber to be used for the new temple. Platforms had been set up in advance along the way, so that when the Deputy King rested, the timber never touched the ground.

The new *mondop*, or shrine, has since seen many alterations. Today Phra Phuttha Bat and its surroundings present a wonderful sight, especially if one knows something of the history of this most sacred shrine with its footprint, to which every year on the full moon of the third lunar month – *Makha Bucha* Day – thousands of devout Buddhists travel to pay homage to the memory of the Lord Buddha.

# The Story of Manora

Another legend much loved in Thailand is the story of Manora. Like the famous *Ramakian*, *Manora* is often the source of scenes in Thai classical dancing and in shadow-puppetry. Here is a rather condensed version of it.

A hunter once met an old hermit who lived by the edge of a large pond in a forest. The hermit told him about the seven beautiful *"kinnaris,"* or half-bird, half-woman, who lived in heaven but came down once a week to swim in the pond. The hunter was anxious to see the *kinnaris*, so he spent the night in the hermit's hut. Early the next morning he went down to the water's edge, where he hid among the foliage. He was rewarded by seeing the seven beautiful creatures descending from heaven. They detached their wings and tails, hung them on a tree, and then splashed about in the pond.

After they had departed again for heaven, the hunter told the hermit he had decided to catch one of them and present her to the Crown Prince of the land. But the old man laughed scornfully; he said the *kinnaris* lived in a royal palace in heaven above Mount Krailat with their father, the king. The only way to catch one, he said, was with a magic serpent, the *"naga* rope."

Luckily the hunter and the King of the *nagas* (*Phya Nak* in Thai) were old friends. The hunter went to see him and was able to borrow a *"naga* rope." He took it back with him to the pond, and waited.

Again the seven beauties flew down and swam in the pond. The hunter cast the *naga* rope at the most beautiful *kinnaree*, Manora, and it coiled itself round her body. "Help! Save me!" she cried in despair. The hunter emerged from the bushes, put Manora's wings and tail in his shoulder-bag, and promised to take her to his prince. The *naga* uncoiled itself and slipped into the hunter's bag.

Terrified, Manora took off her jewelry and hung it on a tree so that her sisters could find it. Then she followed the hunter, and later that day they met the Prince, *Phra* Suthon, riding his elephant. The hunter gave Manora to him, and the Prince carried her back to the city.

The Prince's parents, King Athit and his Queen, were delighted to have a daughter-in-law from heaven. They gave her fine clothes to wear, and Prince *Phra* Suthon was so kind to her and his deep love for her was so evident that Manora soon forgot her grief at being abducted.

One day a courtier asked the Prince's permission to marry the Lord Chamberlain's daughter. The Prince agreed, but the Lord Chamberlain was furious at not being consulted first; he considered this a great insult. He soon found a chance to revenge his injured dignity.

Hearing about Prince Suthon's beautiful wife from heaven, the king of a neighboring country became jealous and coveted her for himself. He sent a vast army to capture her. The cunning Lord Chamberlain told King Athit that only Prince Suthon himself was valiant enough to lead the King's army into battle. His plan worked, and after the Prince had duly gone to war, the black-hearted official put the next step into operation: He told King Athit that all the country's troubles were due to one person only – Manora – and that she should be sacrificed by burning at the stake. Although the King knew that Manora was really a good-hearted girl, he eventually agreed to do this.

However, a palace maid overheard the King's conversation with the Lord Chamberlain, and told Manora the whole story. Poor Manora rushed to the Queen for solace and help. The Queen in her turn went and tried to see the King and make him change his mind; but the guards refused to allow her into the King's room.

The two women wept bitterly. Manora's thoughts flew to her beloved Prince Suthon, far away at the battle-front and unable to protect her. Finally Manora thought of a secret plan.

"I am not afraid to die," she said to the Queen. "But first, let me dance for you. Please give me my wings and tail."

The Queen had never before seen Manora dance as she used to do in heaven. Manora performed her most beautiful and graceful dance while the Queen and all her servants watched, entranced.

The dance went on and on... and then all of a sudden Manora flew away out of the window, high into the sky. (This particular episode is the one often performed by Thai classical dancers.)

"Come back, come back, Manora!" shouted the Queen. But Manora called back that much as she loved her Prince and her parents-in-law, she would return to her home in heaven rather than die at the stake. Her last words were: "Don't let Prince Suthon try to follow me. The way is dangerous, and no human can reach me. Goodbye! I shall always remember your kindness." And then she was gone.

Not long afterwards Prince Suthon won the war and returned home. He looked forward eagerly to seeing his beautiful *kinnari* wife, Manora, again. Back at the palace, he went to greet his parents. To his surprise, he found the King silent and morose: It was the Queen who told him the whole sad story of Manora's departure and the reasons for it.

At first Prince Suthon was overcome with grief and anger. Finally he determined, in spite of Manora's warning, to go in search of her. The Queen pleaded with him, telling him of all the dangers inherent in the journey, but the Prince's mind was made up. He told her he was so broken-hearted that if he did not go, he would die of grief. So the young man set off alone.

First he sought out the hunter, who told him about the hermit and the pond where he had first found Manora. Then he went to find the hermit.

"What is your name?" the old man asked him. "And why have you come? Aren't you afraid of evil spirits?"

Prince Suthon told the hermit who he was, and that he was searching for Manora. "Ah, yes," said the hermit, "she stopped here on her way home, and said you must not try to follow her: Mount Krailat is far, and you would die before you ever reached it. You must go home."

But Prince Suthon was more grimly determined than ever to do no such thing, and said so. Observing with a sigh the Prince's steadfastness of purpose, the hermit gave him Manora's ring and shawl. He also taught him a protective magic spell and gave him some other useful advice. Prince Suthon thanked the old man and went on his way.

Many and terrifying were the obstacles which Prince Suthon met, as Manora and the hermit had warned him. But one by one he overcame them. He wrapped Manora's shawl round himself to disguise himself as a wild animal, and was then snatched up by a huge bird and transported over an otherwise impenetrable mountain. Later he met thousands of poisonous snakes, but the old hermit's magic spell produced a spurt of flame along the edge of the mountain and drove the snakes off.

He came to a river so wide that the opposite bank was out of sight in the distance. But he saw a very large snake lying in the water, and remembered that the hermit had told him he must walk along the snake's back to cross the river while meditating on loving-kindness. In this way the Prince at last reached the far bank safely.

Sitting at the foot of another mountain at dusk, Prince Suthon overheard two giant birds talking in a tree above him.

They were planning to fly to the *kinnarees'* domain the following day, where there was to be a party to welcome Manora back. Later that night, when the two birds were asleep, the Prince climbed up the tree and onto the back of one of the birds. Hanging on tight to the creature's feathers, Prince Suthon waited for dawn.

As the sun rose, the two birds flew high into heaven, then dropped down into the *kinnarees'* royal domain. A maidservant was drawing water for Princess Manora's bath, and Prince Suthon unobtrusively dropped Manora's ring into the pail. When the servant tipped the water into the bath where Manora was sitting, the ring magically slid onto her finger, much to her astonishment.

The servant told Manora that a young man clothed in rags had talked to her while she was drawing the water; in spite of his apparent poverty the stranger was handsome and had noble features. Manora felt certain that this could be none other than her husband.

Manora's father, the King, knew that no human could come to heaven – yet here, according to his daughter, was a young man who had done so. He must surely be highly talented. So Prince Suthon was given fine clothes and invited to Manora's welcome-home party. "Pick out Manora from among my seven *kinnaree* daughters," the King told him. "If you are really her husband, you must know which of them is she."

Seven stunningly lovely *kinnarees* sat facing Prince Suthon – and they all seemed exactly alike! But finally he pointed to one of them, and it was, indeed, his beloved Manora.

After being reunited with her and living happily in heaven

for some time, Prince Suthon asked permission to take Manora to his own land on earth and live with his parents, King Athit and his Queen. This permission was granted. After they had arrived, Manora graciously asked King Athit to pardon the wicked Lord Chamberlain who had caused all the trouble, and spare his life. So instead of executing him, the King had him put on a ship and sent in exile to a distant island.

And as in all fairy stories, in Thailand as in the West, Prince Suthon and his Manora lived happily ever after.

## The Dog Star and the Chick Star

There are two legends about stars in Thailand. One of them is about Sirius, the dog star, and the other about the cluster of seven stars known in the West as the Pleiades.

Sirius is often known in Thai as *dao ma lap*: the "sleeping dog" star. There is a Thai reason for that, too. Sirius is believed to be the type of star known as *dao chon*, or a "robber-star." A baby born at the time Sirius comes up may perhaps become a member of a robber gang. The practical connection with robbers, or more correctly with burglars, or *khamoi*, is that Thais believe when the "sleeping dog" star rises in the sky, all dogs – even house dogs and watchdogs – fall fast asleep and are not easily awakened. So that is the most favorable time to burgle a house, factory, or whatever.

The other star group, the Pleiades, is known in Thai as *dao luk kai*: "the chick star." A baby born at the time when the moon passes *dao luk kai* will have good luck, because this is an auspicious star cluster.

Greek mythology says the seven stars in the Pleiades are the seven daughters of Atlas and Pleione. Thai mythology has a different version, which I will now relate.

An elderly couple went to live in a forest. They built their humble home near a hill, and managed to keep body and soul together by growing a few vegetables and raising chickens. But they were so poor that they possessed only one mother hen, which nevertheless produced seven chicks. They were sturdy and robust little birds, always scrapping and fighting among themselves. The old couple hoped in due course to rear the seven chicks into fine plump hens.

One evening a monk making a journey on foot approached the old couple's home and dropped in for a chat. They welcomed him gladly, as all Buddhists would do. They gave him water to drink and to wash his feet, and invited him to spend the night with them; and he accepted. However, they offered him no food that evening, knowing that monks may not eat after midday until after daybreak the following day.

After the monk had retired for the night and was asleep, the old couple sat whispering. "Whatever shall we give the monk for food tomorrow morning?" they wondered. "We are so poor, there is nothing at all we can give him. But we simply must offer him something, to make merit. And it must be the best food we can possibly find."

They finally decided there was nothing for it: The only way was to kill their mother hen, roast it, and offer it to the monk.

The hen, however, overheard their conversion. Weeping, she gathered her seven chicks under her wing and told them sadly that from now on they must look after themselves. "Now, you must stop fighting one another, and try to love one another," she told them. Pointing to the eldest with her wing, she said, "And you must look after your younger brothers and sisters. Now, all of you please be good little chicks and behave yourselves properly after I'm gone."

Very early next morning the old man built a huge bonfire out of dry twigs. Then with a sorrowful heart he killed the mother hen and put her on the fire to roast. Whereupon the seven chicks were so grief-stricken that they all jumped into the fire, too, and perished as their mother had done.

The seven chicks were reborn as stars in the sky – the cluster of seven stars which Westerners call the Pleiades, and Thais call *dao luk kai*.

## More Local Legends

To end this chapter, here are three more well-known Thai legends. First comes the tale of *Chao Mae* Sao Hai. As I have already mentioned, *Chao Mae* means a female spirit or goddess, and Sao Hai is the name of a village situated on a canal not far from the provincial town of Saraburi.

The local legend is that one day a log came floating along the canal and came to rest in the village of Sao Hai. At first no one paid it any attention, but that night the villagers heard a woman's voice crying "Help!" The voice seemed to be coming from the direction of the log.

Next day a group of the strongest men in the village tried to pull the log out of the water, but they could not budge it.

A few nights later one of the villagers dreamt that a woman came to see him, pleading for his help. She said she was imprisoned in the log and badly wanted to get out. If he could help her, she would bring him great wealth.

Next morning that villager tied a sacred white *sai sin* cord round the log. After prostrating himself and worshipping, the villager found to his great delight that he was able to pull the log out of the canal by means of the white cord with no effort at all.

The goddess who dwelt inside the log kept the promise she had made in the villager's dream. Before long he became rich. *Chao Mae* Sao Hai is still worshipped in the village of that name near Saraburi.

✳

Next comes a fable about the founding of Thailand's former capital, Ayutthaya.

There once lived a man by the name of Saen Pom, which means "a hundred thousand swellings." His face and body were covered with ugly red welts. He was a poor farmer, and grew chilies and eggplants beside the river. His eggplants were the largest in the neighborhood because he fertilized them with his own urine.

One day the daughter of King Trai Treung fancied some eggplants for her supper and sent her servant out to buy some. Knowing that Saen Pom's eggplants were the largest, the servant bought some for the princess, who ate them. Nine months later the princess gave birth to a baby boy.

In reply to her father's repeated questioning, the princess stuck firmly to her assertion that she had never been with any man. Later on, when the boy was about two years old, the King, anxious to find out who the boy's father was, summoned a meeting of all the local men. He commanded that each man should bring some fruit or a cake with him. All the men were to assemble in front of the palace gates.

When every man had arrived, the King made a prayer that the infant prince would identify his father by taking the fruit or cake from him. Then he let the little boy run freely among the assembled men. Saen Pom was there, holding a handful of cold rice. As soon as the little prince saw him, he ran straight up to him.

So the King's prayer was answered; the boy had indeed identified his father. But the King was greatly grieved to find that the father was not only poor but disfigured as well. However, he gave his daughter and little grandson to Saen Pom, and they went to live with him on his humble farm.

The green god Indra saw that the "miracle" birth of the princess' child was causing anguish to three humans; so he came down to earth disguised as a monkey. He gave Saen Pom a drum, telling him to beat the drum whenever he needed anything and his wish would be granted.

Saen Pom was overjoyed, for he had always been deeply troubled by his unsightly body. He struck the drum, and was immediately changed into a handsome man.

Out of gratitude, he built a cradle of pure gold for his infant son, and named him Phrachao U-Thong, which means "Prince of the Golden Cradle."

He then struck the drum once more, praying that a township might spring up around his farm. This wish, too, was granted. The town was named U Thong (as it still is today) and when the little prince grew up, he became King U-Thong. After his father, Saen Pom, died, King U-thong (who later became King Rama Thibodi I) founded the capital city of Ayutthaya. This, then, is the well-known tale of how Ayutthaya came to be founded.

❉

Near Ayutthaya is the former summer royal palace of Bang Pa-In. Here is the legend of how it got its name.

Many years ago a certain king who liked to travel incognito among his subjects visited Ayutthaya Province disguised as a local man. The King's boat overturned, and he swam to an island. He spent the night in a villager's hut with a girl called "In," the villager's daughter. Next morning he took his leave of her, but first he gave her a ring. "If ever you need my help," he said, "you may come to the Royal Palace. Show this ring to the guard at the gate, and he will bring you to see me."

A year later, the girl named In followed the King's suggestion. She now had a tiny baby on her arm, and needed money to rear him. Showing her baby to the King, she discreetly indicated that the King was its father, whereupon he gave her some money, but told her she could not stay in the palace.

After In and her baby had gone, the King pondered long over what she had told him. He found it very hard to believe that the child was really his. He asked one of his courtiers how he could father a child after spending only one night with the girl. Afraid of giving offence, the courtier resorted to an old Thai proverb. "Your Majesty," he said, "if the tree is strong, it can indeed bear fruit after only one pollination."

The King was impressed by this diplomatic answer: It convinced him that In had told the truth. So he gave orders that henceforth the place where he had met her should be called "The Village where I met In" – in Thai, Bang Pa-In.

As for the baby boy, he eventually became King Prasat Thong, who founded the Palace at Bang Pa-In.

# CHAPTER SEVEN

# families

## How Family Relationships Are Expressed in Thai

In the section on the Thai word *khun* in Chapter 4, I mentioned the Thai words *phi* and *nong*. *Phi* is used as a polite way of addressing an older friend, but its actual meaning is "elder brother or sister." Similarly, *nong* is used when speaking to a younger friend (or occasionally by that younger friend to mean "I" when talking to an older friend), but its real meaning is "younger brother or sister."

These two words – *phi* for an older brother or sister, and *nong* for a younger one – can apply to either sex, and can be used on their own, without specifying which sex is meant. They can also be qualified by adding the endings -*chai* (male) or -*sao* (female), to make the words *phi-chai* (elder brother), *nong-chai* (younger brother), *phi-sao* (elder sister), and *nong-sao* (younger sister). Thus the primary emphasis in brother/sister relationships in Thai is on age rather than sex; whereas in English (and, I imagine, all other European languages) it is the other way round. The English words "brother" and "sister" tell us nothing at all about age, and they must therefore be qualified by adding "elder" or "younger." This difference highlights the great importance attached to seniority in Thailand – a subject I also dealt with in Chapter 4.

## Phi and Nong

But there is more to those words *phi* and *nong*. Firstly, when a Thai refers to his *phi-chai*, *nong-chai*, and so on, he may not actually mean a blood brother or sister, or even a half-brother; it may be a cousin, or some other person who has lived as a member of his family since he was a child, and whom he therefore thinks of as an elder/younger brother/sister, as the case may be.

Secondly, the *phi-nong* seniority relationship can affect the way in which cousins are referred to. Suppose your cousin is younger than you, but his/her father or mother is older than yours; you call that cousin *phi* to indicate the age relationship between your respective parents. But this custom is slowly dying out, so I am told.

Lastly, *phi* is often used by a husband to refer to himself when speaking to his wife, and by his wife when addressing her husband or referring to him in conversation with someone else. Conversely, *nong* is used in the same way by a wife to refer to herself when speaking to her husband, and by the husband when addressing his wife. When a man calls his wife *nong*, it conveys the feeling of "dear" or "darling."

## Grandparents, Uncles, and Aunts

When we come to grandparents, uncles, and aunts, the various Thai words convey much more information than the corresponding English ones – once you know them and can remember them! In English, if we talk about our grandmother and we want to be more specific, we must either say "my father's mother" or the equally clumsy "my grandmother on my father's side," and, correspondingly, if we mean "on my mother's side." In Thai, one's father's mother is simply *yah* and one's mother's mother is *yai*. One's grandfather on the father's side is *pu*, and grandfather on the mother's side is *ta*. Much easier than English, isn't it?

The words for uncles and aunts are a bit more complicated, but each of them carries an almost computer-like mass of information. Nah means a younger brother or sister of one's mother. So *na-chai* means "an uncle, a younger brother of one's mother," and *na-sao* is the corresponding kind of aunt. *Ah* means the same thing all over again, but on one's father's side: So *ah-chai* means that particular kind of uncle, and *ah-sao*, ditto for aunt.

If the uncle or aunt is older than one's father or mother, the information carried by the Thai, word is slightly less: *Pa* is an aunt who is an elder sister of either one's father or mother, while *lung* is the corresponding type of uncle. (My stepson, Jiap, always refers to me as *khun lung*.)

I hope all that is quite clear!

## Papa and Mama

After all those different kinds of uncles and aunts, it is a relief to get back to two of the most fundamental words in the world. In Victorian England children in polite society called their parents "Papa" and "Mama." "He calls his mother his ma" ran an old English music-hall song, and "Pa" and "Ma" are still used in some parts of Britain. In the United States there are two familiar forms: "Pop" and "Mom," and "Paw" and "Maw."

And what are the words in Thai? Why, *Pho* and *Mae*, which is pronounced "Mair." These, of course, are all popular forms used by children. We also have two formal words in English: Father and mother. These words are directly related to the Latin words *pater* and *mater*. And those Latin words are in turn related to the Sanskrit words *pita* and *mata*. From these two Sanskrit words have come the formal Thai words for "father" and "mother": *bida* and *manda*.

It's a small world, isn't it?

# Family Life

The spirit of family solidarity is a cornerstone of Thai society. Thai family life is on the whole far more closely knit than is usual in the West. One of the main factors forming these strong bonds of attachment is the universal love and respect for parents and older relatives: The difference and homage shown to seniority, summed up in all those various words for relatives – *phi* and *nong, ya* and *yai, pu* and *ta*, all those complex but precise words for different kinds of uncles and aunts – and *Pho* and *Mae*.

Another word I have not yet mentioned is *lan*. This is a bit more ambiguous, because it can mean "grandchild," "nephew, niece," or even "second cousin," depending on the context. As with *phi* and *nong*, sex is indicated by the suffix: *lan-chai* is male, *lan-sao* female. I sometimes find difficulty in explaining in Thai to casual acquaintances that I have a grandson and granddaughter in England from my first marriage. They get the impression that I am referring to a nephew and niece. I have to say *pen pu laeo* ("I am a grandfather on my son's side already"), and then make doubly sure by adding *khao pen luk khong luk-chai* – "they are the children of my son."

To return to the topic of Thai family life, when a young man marries, the couple often goes to live with the bride's parents, along with all her brothers, sisters, and their spouses. Sometimes they all live together in one big house; or they may each have their own separate houses within the family compound. I have never quite understood why it is more often the bride's parents' property; but that certainly seems to be the Thai tradition.

The young couple move in with their parents out of a desire to look after the older folk. By so doing they gain merit; and a bit later on there is a more immediate advantage – instant, constantly available and free baby-sitting! The young wife's mother looks after the babies while her daughter goes out to work, to parties, and even on a trip to the provinces or abroad.

The very real feeling of togetherness within the Thai family circle is called *unchai* – literally "heartwarming," or conveying a sense of security. If any member of the family is in financial trouble, the resources of the whole family are mobilized to provide help; if someone is ill, there is always some other family member to look after them.

Married couples who do not live with their families usually go to their parents' home every year on *Songkran* Day in mid-April (the ancient Thai New Year). They bring presents of cloth to make sarongs, and sprinkle perfumed water over their parents as an act of homage. The parents in their turn wish blessings on their children.

Thais who have children need never worry about saving up for their old age. They know with certainty that their children will never let them starve, but will continue to support them out of gratitude for their rearing, upbringing, and education.

# Laddawan

My wife's family history is probably typical of many families in rural Thailand, and her grandmother's twenty-six grandchildren span a wide range of society from university professor to illiterate servant.

By all accounts Laddawan's grandmother seems to have been quite a character. It was she who brought up Laddawan and her sister from babyhood after their mother died. Although not badly off – her husband had owned large coconut orchards just outside Bangkok – Grandmother was inclined to be on the stingy side. She used to roll up her 100-baht notes so tightly that they were almost the thickness of a matchstick, and stow them away in the hidden pocket of her country-style shoulder-vest, presumably to outwit pickpockets. One cannot blame her really, considering that one hundred baht fifty years ago was probably worth at least 5,000 baht today, if not more.

Grandmother was extremely religious, and always knew when a *wan phra*, or Buddhist holy day, came round every eight days or so. In those days the Western months and days of the week went unheeded among country folk, and as a child Laddawan had barely heard of Monday, Tuesday, and so on. On every *wan phra* day Grandmother went to the local temple, Wat Suan Som, or the Orange Grove Temple, to make merit. While there she very sensibly took the opportunity to scrape up the "candle tear-drops," as the Thais so picturesquely call them – the candle-grease droppings on the temple floor. Back home she melted this down in hot water and rolled it into cylindrical sticks. This saved her having to buy candles.

Grandmother had six daughters. Their subsequent fortunes, not unnaturally, depended almost entirely on the kind of marriages they made.

The eldest daughter married a very poor man. One of their children fell down a few steps at the age of six months and permanently injured her back. The little girl grew up a hunchback; it hurt her to sit upright for long periods, so she was excused from attending school. As a result, this cousin of Laddawan's is now illiterate. She was at one time our maid, and was a very good cook, too; but housework naturally soon tired her.

Each of the other five daughters produced offspring according to their various social stations. One of the sons of daughter number five obtained his Ph.D. degree in Europe and is now an associate professor in one of Thailand's major universities. Some of Laddawan's other cousins are in the police, military, and government service.

Laddawan's own mother was Grandmother's youngest daughter. She died when Laddawan was only a year old and her sister two years old. The little girls' father was quite poor and refused to have anything to do with their upbringing. So for the first twelve years or so Grandmother took care of them.

A small *khlong*, or canal, ran along the bottom of Grandmother's garden, and as toddlers Laddawan and her sister used to play along the edge. From time to time one or other of the little girls fell into the canal, and would certainly have drowned if it had not been for Grandmother. Each time one of them fell in the water, that intrepid lady, already in her sixties, dashed to the rescue, jumping in fully clothed and fishing the child out from a watery death.

When they were about nine years old, the two little girls enjoyed a sport popular with children wherever there is tidal water in Thailand. They waited for low tide, when the canal drained dry and the muddy banks were exposed. In the banks were many holes, inside which were tasty crabs and various kinds of small edible fish. Each of these holes has two entrances – a front door and a back door, so to speak. The way to catch the tasty morsel is to plunge both hands in at the same time, one into each of the two entrances, grab the fish by its head or tail and pull it out. Laddawan and her sister did this for hours on end at low tide. Until one day Laddawan put her hands into a pair of holes and pulled out a snake! She let go with a loud shriek- and that was definitely the last time either of them indulged in that particular sport.

Laddawan still has some scars on her hands produced by mishandling a knife in the dark during her teens. No, not armed robbery or anything like that! Simply gathering co-conut-palm sugar. When she was about fourteen, Laddawan and her sister had to get up before dawn every day to col-lect the sugar from the 170 palm trees in Grandmother's orchard – a rather dangerous process calling for skill and steady nerves.

Long ladders were fixed firmly and permanently to each tree. Each ladder consisted of a single central bamboo pole more than thirty feet long and about six inches in diam-eter. Thin wooden rungs stuck out on either side of the stout central pole.

At four or five a.m. the two teenage girls would go out into the orchard. Each of them carried a kerosene lamp, a sharp machete-like knife tucked inside her belt, and thirty to forty hollow sections of bamboo called *krabok*, each about a foot long, as collecting-vessels for the sugar. They carried these *krabok* on shoulder-poles like those of street vendors.

Each girl climbed up a ladder, carrying her lamp and one *krabok*. When she was high enough to reach the palm flower containing the sugar, she perched precariously with one foot on a rung and the other leg hooked round the central pole of the ladder, so that both her arms were free. The lamp was hung on a higher rung of the ladder. The *krabok*, which had already been attached beneath the flower the previous day, and which was now more than half full of the pale yellow liquid sugar, was removed.

Now came the really difficult bit. The tip of the pointed flower had to be sliced off with that sharp dangerous knife – rather like tapping a rubber tree. In the dark, the knife sometimes hit the wrong target; that is how Laddawan got those scars on her hands. (Sometimes it was not because of the dark, but due to carelessness while she was gossiping with a neighbor on top of a ladder in the next orchard!)

The fresh empty *krabok* was now fixed in position under the flower, with the newly cut tip just inside the vessel so that the syrupy liquid could drip into it. And so, down the ladder again and on to the next tree. It took the two girls about three hours to cover the seventy trees in the orchard.

On the way back to the house, of course, those thirty or forty *krabok* slung on the shoulder-poles were now considerably heavier with their load of palm-sugar. In the house, the liquid sugar was boiled in a large metal vat until it became sticky, after which it was churned until solid – another tough job needing two people. Have you ever tasted coconut palm-sugar? It is delicious – rather like fudge.

The sugar was, of course, sold. As everyone in the village knew everyone else, no shop or stall was necessary for this;

most of the customers were Grandmother's friends who used to drop by whenever they needed some sugar. All that hard and dangerous work for six hundred baht a month for each girl! But twenty-five years ago the baht was a very different currency from today.

Laddawan has perhaps even more than her share of the delightful Thai sense of humor. She enjoys taking liberties with the English language, even though she has far from mastered it. For instance: "I'll do it tomorrow, or if not, then three-morrow!"

Recently she has accused me, not without good reason, of becoming a bit lazy, something like Andy Capp, I suppose, because at weekends I tend to loll back in a chair with my feet up and ask her to bring this or fetch that. The other day she came out with two rather salty rural Thai expressions for this; translated into English, these are roughly "Your posterior has grown roots," and "your posterior is sticking to the floor boards!"

But I think our biggest-ever laugh was many years ago when Laddawan asked me what "motorball" meant. I said I had never heard of it, whereupon she sang the opening words of a then current hit, "Tell Laura I Love Her," which are:

"Tommy and Laura were lovers.
He wanted to give her everything –
Flowers . . . present . . . but MOTORBALL
A wedding ring . . . "

It was quite a few moments before I recovered my composure enough to explain that the correct words were "Most of all" . . .

# CHAPTER EIGHT
# Thai fortune-telling

## It's in the Cards

Fortune-telling is probably as popular in Thailand as anywhere in the world. A dozen or so different methods are used, and you may be sure that one of the commonest is "What's in the cards?"

The card method I am going to describe is used by many Thai people. My wife uses it constantly – on friends, on myself, and in the absence of anyone else, on herself. This method can be surprisingly accurate, but it is also very short-term; predictions are reliable only up to a week or so ahead, or a fortnight at most. I asked my wife to tell my fortune so I could write about it. Here is how it is done.

First, all the sixes and lower cards are removed from the pack. The pack that remains consists of thirty-two cards. Aces are high. Generally speaking, red cards are good and black ones bad, but there are exceptions to this rule, depending on their position relative to other cards.

The King of Diamonds, representing me, was removed from the pack and placed face upwards in the middle of the table. (If I were fatter than I am, the King of Hearts would be used; for men under thirty, the corresponding Jacks are used, and for women, of course, the Queens.)

I then shuffled the pack, made a *wai* for good luck by holding the pack between my flattened palms and raising them towards my face, after which I cut the pack. My wife offered me the cards face downwards, spread out in a fan. I picked one at random, and this was placed face downwards covering the King of Diamonds. My wife then dealt out the cards face upwards in a pattern like eight spokes of a wheel, with the King of Diamonds and its covering card at the center. She started by making a cross, then filled in the diagonal "spokes." This is always done in clockwise order for a man, anti-clockwise for a woman. The spaces between the "spokes" were filled with more cards.

Out of the remaining six face-downwards cards I now chose three. (Not much of a choice really, but that is how it is.) My wife inspected the three cards I had chosen, together with the card which had been laid face downwards on the King of Diamonds.

After she had studied the whole pattern of cards carefully, her predictions began. A dark person would make a lot of trouble for me. I must watch my health carefully. I would also receive bad news from a dark woman, and would make a journey to somewhere I had not been before. On the plus side, a white-skinned younger man would give me some money. This came true! (I think he owed it to me, anyway.)

The cards were swept back into a pack ready for stage two. Shuffle, *wai*, and cut again. This time the cards were laid out in four rows of eight cards each.

The eight vertical columns of this pattern, starting from the left, refer to *ngeon, ngan, rak, mit, thi-yu, kan doen thang, plian plaeng yok yai, samret* – or in English, money, job, love, friendship, home, travel, change, and success.

There would be a change for the better, my wife announced, after inspecting this pattern carefully. The King of Diamonds, still representing me, was in the last column but one, the "change" column, and the seven of hearts in the same column meant good luck. But beware of a false friend, a woman: The Queen of Clubs in the "friendship" column. Money would be good: The seven and eight of diamonds in the first column spelled financial help from someone. (The same white-skinned young man, perhaps?) Work would also be good, with something new happening, as indicated by the nine of diamonds in the second column. A nine means something new, probably because the poetic Thai word *nawa* means both "nine" and "new." But the three black cards sitting side-by-side at the left of the bottom row signified some bad news. Travel would be good, as shown by the nine of hearts in the "travel" column. Spades seem to be high the world over. The Queen of Spades in the "success" column meant a woman of high position would bring me good luck.

For the third time I shuffled, made a *wai*, and cut the pack. The top six cards were placed in two rows of three in the middle of the table. Groups of cards representing the next eight days were placed round them, in anti-clockwise order.

The prediction from this pattern was that I would have guests the following day, a Sunday (a fact which we both knew already). On the Monday, three aces in a line showed I would get good news from a stranger, a man. On Tuesday, I would receive some money from a dark man, as indicted by the ten of hearts. (The red tens mean receiving money; the black ones, spending or losing it.) On Thursday, I would discuss work, represented by the seven of clubs, and on Friday I would again meet someone new, to my advantage (a red nine again). Saturday and the following Sunday were a mass of black cards – I had better be careful. (I was. I sat in a deck-chair all day. Nothing much happened, apart from mosquito bites.)

# Your Future is in Your Hands!

Telling fortunes by palmistry can be a thriving and lucrative business in Thailand. A few years ago Laddawan went with a friend to have her fortune told by a well-known Bangkok palmist, *Nai* (Mr.) Kom Lertsawai. While examining her hand, *Nai* Kom spotted a very rare and special line on it -the *yan* line. *Yan* (I have spelt it more or less phonetically) means something like "intuition, insight or instinct." Anyone who has this line on his or her hand has special intuitive powers, and *Nai* Kom therefore suggested that Laddawan should study palmistry seriously and then take it up professionally.

Laddawan, however, disagreed. Throughout her whole life, she and education have never been good friends. No matter whether at school, or learning typing (she was a dropout after a month), or learning TV and radio repair (that lasted a year – but at least she can now use a soldering iron!), Laddawan and learning simply were not meant for each other – that was the way she felt.

Her friends egged her on to follow the palmist's advice because they all knew from first-hand experience (pardon the pun) that she really does have some kind of a knack with palm-reading. But the harder they urged her, the more determined Laddawan became to have nothing to do with it. She simply was not interested, and that was that.

Then, after a year or so, she began having second thoughts. There might be something in the idea after all, and the thought of all the lovely money she could earn certainly made it seem rather tempting, even if it did mean doing some more learning.

Then I stepped into the picture and started encouraging her. I offered to pay for her lessons. That did it. Off she went.

Her teacher, *Nai* Kom, has had quite an interesting life so far. The son of a well-to-do Thonburi rice merchant, he is No. 4 in a family of ten children. At the age of sixteen he joined his father's business. He was very fond of sports, especially Thai boxing, which he learnt in the evenings at Wat Buranawas, the local temple.

One evening an old Chinese sage who lived at the temple and often watched young Kom practising his boxing, called him over. He examined Kom's hand, and also studied his general appearance and manner (this is a kind of fortune-telling known as *du laksana* in Thai and *ngo heng* in Chinese). The old man made three important predictions about Kom's future. Firstly, he advised Kom in the strongest possible terms not to take up boxing as a profession, because he would not be successful. Secondly, he said that at the age of eighteen Kom would learn carpentry, and would continue as a carpenter until he was thirty-five. Lastly, at the age of thirty-five Kom must set up his own fortune-telling business, at which he would be very successful and famous.

"Would you like to start learning fortune-telling right away?" the old sage asked him. "I'll teach you, if you like!" Kom agreed at once, and started lessons the next evening. He continued for the next two years, until the old man died.

When Kom was eighteen, his father's rice business started going downhill, so the young man crossed the Chao Phya River and began looking for work in Bangkok. Quite by chance he met a friend who had his own furniture business, and so . . . . Yes, Kom became a furniture-maker, just as the old Chinese had foretold. And, again true to prediction, he continued in his friend's furniture business until he was thirty-five, at which time that too started losing money, and Kom had to leave.

Again purely by chance Kom got into conversation with a

stranger on a train, an army sergeant-major. As you have probably guessed by now, the sergeant-major was also an expert in . . . palmistry. His name was Suchat Suprasoet, and he told Kom he was giving a lecture on palmistry that same day to the Thai Astrologers' Association. He invited Kom to come along. From that day on, Suchat (who is now an *Achan*, or lecturer, in palmistry) became Kom's teacher. So Kom became an expert palmist, and the third and final prediction made by the old Chinese came true.

Some years ago Mr. Kom and *Achan* Suchat were asked to give a joint lecture to the staff at Phra Mongkut Klao Hospital. *Achan* Bunchuei, then President of the Thai Astrologers' Association, was in the chair.

After the lecture was over, one of the hospital doctors brought in six patients, all suffering from different diseases. In front of a packed audience of medical staff, the doctor challenged Mr. Kom and *Achan* Suchat to diagnose each patient's illness. By studying the patients' hands, the two palmists were able to state correctly exactly what disease each person was suffering from. This feat greatly impressed the audience.

Not long afterwards Nat Kom and *Achan* Suchat started up in business under the name of "Supaloet Fortune-tellers." The name Supaloet is a combination of both men's surnames, but it also means "excellent luck."

The name seems to have been aptly chosen. Plenty of customers come to see Nat Kom at the "shop" every day. Many of them are "regulars" who tell their friends, and so business prospers. Most of the customers are women. Sometimes Nat Kom visits his wealthier clients in their own offices or homes.

*Nai* Kom certainly has good reason to feel grateful to the

old Chinese sage at the temple who predicted his future correctly all those years ago. . . .

In Thai, any fortune-teller is called a *mo du*, literally a "look-doctor," and palmistry is called *du lai mue*: "Looking at the lines on the hand."

The whole of Thai palmistry is closely connected with astrology, as I suppose it is everywhere. In order for Laddawan to analyse the lines on a person's hand, especially if they are not clear or sharp, she likes to know that person's basic astrological birth data: Place of birth, date, year, day of the week, and especially the time of birth. The more precisely the time is known, the more accurate the prediction will be.

Taking palm-prints is more accurate than simply examining a person's hands. The small, fine lines show up much more clearly. To make the prints, the two palms are smeared liberally with printer's ink, and each hand in turn is then pressed down firmly and steadily (so as not to blur the fine lines) on a sheet of paper. People are sometimes afraid they will not be able to get the ink off their hands afterwards, but it is easily removed with soap or detergent and water.

Did you know that the lines on your hands gradually change after a period of time? Laddawan says one ought to have one's palm read every two months or so – or at least every six months, like visiting the dentist (only it does not hurt so much).

However, there are three major lines which all people have on their hands throughout their life, and these usually change only very little during the course of a year or so. In Thai these three lines are called *sen prathan*, or "president lines" (sounds like a shipping company, doesn't it?). These lines are the heart line, the brain line, and the life line. Tiny lines may sometimes sprout sideways from these big lines, appearing and disappearing as time goes by.

The life lines on both my hands are long, signifying long life; they are also thin, but sharp and clear. This, says Laddawan, means doggedness and an ability to stand up to life's trials and tribulations. On both hands the heart lines are not continuous and are slightly confused, not neat and tidy, not *riap roi* as the Thais say. This means bad luck in affairs of the heart, either spiritual or physical. So I must try to keep my cool at all times. (I do try – not always successfully.)

Both my brain lines are very long. This indicates a good intellect (I'm not making this up; it is what Laddawan says) and a good memory. My comment on this diagnosis is that I sometimes do the daftest things and, as for my memory, I am just about as absent-minded as they come. I have been known to put salt in my coffee, and even strawberry jam on my toothbrush.

The five or so other major lines on my hand and their many smaller tributaries may appear on some people's hands, but not on those of others. Not everyone has the *sen watsana*, or "fate line," running up the middle of the palm towards the middle finger. This tells about good fortune, generally caused by good deeds done in a former existence. Nor does everyone have the "success line" or "sun line" (*sen athit*), which runs roughly parallel to the "fate line", and may start at the heart line (as on my left hand), from the life line (as on my right) or from many other places, finishing at the third finger. Depending on the starting-point of this line, the palmist can predict what type of success will come.

The "fate lines" and "success lines" on both my hands are what Laddawan calls "bright." The fact that I have both these lines on both hands indicates general success in my aims. The strong "fate line" means happiness, success in work, and riches. I suppose the first two are more or less true, but as for the third – roll on the day: Every time the electricity bill comes, I nearly have the heart failure indicated by my heart line!

My "success line" means that no one has power to make really big trouble for me, because up till now at any rate, there are no small lines near the top ("influence-lines") cutting across the "success line." I hope my wife 's right about that; and, to be honest, I believe she is. Apart from a more or less permanent shortage of baht, things have not gone too badly for me, touch wood... The short lines running up from the brain line to the base of the forefinger on both hands are called "Jupiter lines" or "progress lines." Apparently not everyone has these lines either (Laddawan has not got them yet, but she is hoping they will come).

The labyrinth of lines on different people's hands can vary greatly in shape and direction, with all manner of resultant meanings concerning a person's character and future. In general, lines going up and down the hand are good, while those going across the hand horizontally are bad. Looking at the smaller lines, triangles, and squares on my hand, Laddawan says *mue suai* – a nice-looking hand.

It looks just like any other hand to my untutored eye.

## Will Your Dreams Come True?

One night my wife dreamt I was dead. She seemed very pleased about it, and told me her dream will add another seven years to my life. I hope she is right. This is a very common belief in Thailand. Laddawan can sometimes forecast people's future from their dreams. Some of her knowledge comes from folklore, ancient superstitions handed down by word of mouth over the centuries, and some of it from books – or rather, from one book in particular, which is full of weird and wonderful dreams and their meanings.

Everyone, says Laddawan, has his or her own personal guardian spirit. When we dream, our guardian spirit is trying to tell us something about our future. This is the essential meaning of all dreams.

The time when the dream occurs is important – if it can be remembered! This tells us how far in the future the event foretold in the dream will take place. A dream between six p.m. and ten p.m. indicates something a long time ahead; between eleven p.m. and two a.m., it means an event in one to three months' time; while if it is after two a.m., the event will occur very soon – within three to fifteen days.

Laddawan's son, my stepson Jiap, dreamt he was driving a car and reached the top of a hill. Any dream of this kind, in which some sort of goal is achieved, such as climbing to the top of a tree, swimming safely across a river or canal, and so on, always means success in real life. The day after Jiap had his dream, Laddawan suddenly saw in the cards (she was telling her own fortune, as she invariably does whenever she has got a fit of the blues) that Jiap was going to get a job. Before the week was out, he actually did get his very first job – to the great delight of all three of us. So the message in the cards confirmed that of the dream, and both of them came true.

In 1977, in the middle of the hot season, Jiap dreamed the fence around our garden was on fire. Laddawan knew this dream meant trouble of some kind. Three weeks later, Jiap went down with typhoid.

Many of the dreams in Laddawan's book mean good fortune, success, fame, power, riches, and so on. Among them are some highly unlikely dreams such as seeing a frog eating the sun or the moon, or – even more unlikely – a dream in which, while eating rice with lotus leaves, you see a serpent AND an elephant!

Other dreams with "lucky" meanings given in the same book are: Buying, selling, or eating a chicken; holding a glass or a key in your hand; seeing or sitting in a horse-drawn or elephant-drawn carriage; holding someone in your arms; opening an umbrella, especially if it is a many-tiered state umbrella; seeing any king or queen; eating any kind of specially delicious food; hearing or seeing someone beating drums; and eating human flesh (how would you like your steak, Sir? Medium rare, please). In particular, if you dream you are eating someone's head (uncooked), you will attain a position of great responsibility with many subordinates working under you.

As with Laddawan's dream about my death, many dreams "go by opposites" – as, indeed, all dreams are supposed to do in the West. For instance, if a close relative or friend is ill, and you dream the illness is getting worse, there will be a complete recovery. If you dream you have been given the sack from your job, you will get promotion. A dream in which someone cuts off your hand means you will receive something of great value, or make a handsome profit on a sale. If you are in the middle of a lawsuit and you dream you have won it, you will in fact lose it, and vice versa.

Dream you are laughing, and you will have reason to cry; but dream you are crying, and you will receive a gift very much to your liking, or successfully revive an old love affair. Dream you are angry with a casual acquaintance, and that person will become your close friend. A dream in which you are put in prison means success in your work and fulfillment of your every wish; and if, besides being in prison, your legs are chained, you will be immune from danger of every kind. As for dreaming you are clutching a worm, maggot, or other slimy creature – that means you are all set to win the lottery!

Not only may our apparently harmless dreams be a warning of impending danger, says my wife, sometimes the dream may itself influence our future. Thai people, not only rural but city folk as well, believe that dreams should always be told to someone who is able to interpret them; and in our own interest, we should do so as soon as possible after the dream. The dream-expert can then tell us what to expect and prepare for. We should never tell our dreams to anyone who lacks the skill to interpret them until we have told them to an expert first.

Two very "powerful" and "bad" dreams are especially well known and recognized in Thailand. Firstly, the dream about fire which I mentioned above: If you dream your house is on fire, this invariably means some kind of trouble or danger at home. If in your dream you manage to put out the fire, this means you will be able to overcome the trouble eventually; but should you fail to put it out, your problem may well prove insuperable.

According to Thai superstition, immediately after we have such a dream we should tell it to the sea-goddess or *Mae* Khongkha, literally "Mother of the Waters." This is because water can put out fire. Because of its great power for evil, we should tell this dream to the "Mother of the Waters" at once, and beg for her help. She has the power to help us overcome whatever trouble is in store. (*Mae* Khongkha is mentioned in Chapter 2, in the section on *Loi Krathong*.) The other powerful and bad dream universally known in Thailand is about back teeth. In English-speaking countries we talk glibly about being "fed up to the back teeth," but here in Thailand it is considered much more serious than that. If you dream one of your back teeth is broken, this means you or some elderly member of your family will die . . . If the tooth is an upper one, the person who dies will be a man; if it is a lower one, it will be a woman.

Just as a dream about climbing to the top of a tree or a mountain, or some similar achievement, is a sure sign of success, so dreams about falling usually mean just the opposite. If you dream you fall out of a tree or out of any kind of vehicle, be it a royal chariot, a buffalo-cart, or even a *samlo*, this means trouble of some kind. A special case is a dream about falling off a buffalo; this means danger from an enemy.

Many other dreams besides the one about back teeth are related to death or sickness. When Laddawan was younger and her ninety-three-year-old grandmother lay slowly dying and unable to move for a period of several weeks, Laddawan dreamt night after night that her grandmother had got up and was doing a very energetic *ramwong*, or some other sprightly dance with great gusto and obvious enjoyment!

Other dreams which foretell death, sickness, or some calamity include those in which the dreamer sees him or herself wearing black, or in which one's foot falls off one's leg or sustains some kind of wound. Dreaming that one is struggling on foot through thick mud means a sudden and unexpected illness; so do dreams in which one breaks a leg, is wearing beautiful clothes, is blind or suffering from poor eyesight, or sees one's own shadow. If you see someone else's shadow in your dream, that other person will become ill – but you will not get off free, as you will be put to some financial expense on their account . . .

If you dream a crocodile is biting you, someone will cheat or betray you. A dream in which you are riding a horse means worry caused by a friend or relative, and one in which you see a thief in your house means someone in your family will involve you in loss of money. Someone will spread malicious gossip about you after you have had a dream in which you are standing on tiptoe.

Other dreams which foretell trouble include seeing the ashes inside a stove, which means bad tidings from far away; finding and keeping something of great value, which means a quarrel with one's wife or husband; and losing a key, which means one will lose money. Dreaming one has reached old age means unexpected trouble, probably in the form of a lawsuit, while a cart passing by in one's dreams foretells sorrow. So does a dream about eating a bird, but with this dream the sorrow will not last long.

A dream about digging in the ground can have two more or less opposite meanings; if the earth underneath is dirty, we can expect trouble from a friend, while if the earth is clean this means good news.

Any dream about a snake is good. This is another universally recognized dream in Thailand. Not a very pleasant dream-subject, you may think. But here in Thailand, dreams about snakes are apparently fairly common, and their general meaning is well understood. If you dream about a snake, it means you will soon meet your *neua khu*, or predestined soul-mate. Thais who tell their friends they have had a dream about a snake are immediately greeted with loud laughter and the usual ribald innuendoes. Even more so if the dreamer happens to be a married man . . . It means he is about to acquire a new *mia noi* (minor wife)!

There are, of course, many variations on the snake-dream theme. For instance, you may dream that a snake bites you, and you strike it and kill it; then, as is the way with dreams, it comes back to life again. This dream means wedding bells for sure (or a new minor wife, as the case may be). Or the dream-snake may coil itself around your body, and so on.

Many of us can remember vividly dreams we have had a long time ago. Laddawan remembers clearly a dream she had as a young girl, in which a small black snake coiled itself tightly around her legs. However hard she tried, she could not pull the snake off. Then a stranger appeared and together they managed to get the snake off her legs. Soon after that dream, Laddawan met her first husband. But the marriage was a failure, and they were soon divorced again. Although she did not realise it at the time, her dream foretold this unhappy outcome too – not because the snake was black, but because it was on the lower part of her body.

Many years later Laddawan had another snake dream. This time she dreamt she was walking and was being followed by a very large white snake, which could not catch up with her. Soon after having that dream, she met me! Evidently something about the snake's size or color, or perhaps the fact that it did not attack her, gave the dream a "good" meaning, and signified a more lasting relationship.

A friend of my wife's had a dream about a green grass-snake (*ngu khiao*) and soon afterwards she met a new boyfriend whose name was . . . Khiao!

As with snakes, so with elephants. If an unmarried woman dreams an elephant twines its trunk around her, this also foretells that her soul-mate is on his way to her, but he will be a widower much older than her, and of high rank and position. If, however, after the elephant has coiled its trunk around her, it batters her repeatedly and painfully on the ground, the elderly widower whom she marries will turn out to be a deceiver, slanderer, and a thoroughly bad lot generally.

Another dream which heralds the imminent arrival of your soul-mate is one in which a leech has attached itself to any part of your body and is sucking away at your blood for all its worth. But this, too, is a bad dream, and the marriage will soon end up on the rocks.

Dreams about pregnancy also concern soul-mates. If an unmarried woman dreams she is pregnant, this again simply means she will soon meet her predestined lover. But if she is already married, the same dream foretells a quarrel with her husband – and perhaps a divorce again.

There are many other kinds of dreams which predict a meeting with one's true love, one's *nuea khu*. A dream in which one is wandering on a mountain side or in a cave means an early marriage, which will be long-lasting and happy. And if you dream you are eating a really delicious cake, or if you find, touch, or wear gold in your dream, you will not only have a happy marriage, but also a very happy family with children whom you will love very much and who will be equally affectionate towards you.

If you dream you are picking a lotus flower, your life-partner will be a very handsome man or beautiful woman, as the case may be. Picking other attractive and scented flowers in your dreams means a soul-mate of high or noble birth – or perhaps a millionaire! A woman who dreams about the type of Malaysian dagger called a *kris* will soon meet a lover, and a dream in which you hold a bird-cage with a bird inside it also indicates a successful marriage.

Now, that's enough about dreams. But while on the general subject of telling fortunes, here is another method which is rather amusing: A nervous tic or twitch! A twitch above your eyebrow means good news, but one below the eye spells trouble. If you have a twitch just above your upper lip, this means you will eat something you like very much; but if the twitch is on your upper right arm (a funny place for a twitch; surely?), you will meet with an accident. Twitching hips also mean trouble.

One day some years ago my wife was aware of a persistent twitching on the . . . er . . . rear portion of her anatomy. She sensed trouble – and sure enough, that night we had burglars!

# Thai Astrology

## (1) Colors of the Day

A very ancient Thai tradition associates a different color with each day of the week, and holds that clothes of the appropriate color should be worn on the correct day. I referred briefly to this in the section on "Lak Mueang" in Chapter 4, in which I said that Thai armies of old had to wear the correct "color of the day" when going into battle. Trying to find out some more about this custom and its origins, I asked my wife as usual. She has a friend who is an experienced astrologer named *Achan* Bunchuei (of whom, more anon). Here is what I found out.

First of all, the colors. These are as follows:

| | | |
|---|---|---|
| Sunday | - | red |
| Monday | - | cream or yellow |
| Tuesday | - | pink |
| Wednesday | - | green |
| Thursday | - | orange or brown |
| Friday | - | blue |
| Saturday | - | black or purple |

These colors are traditionally associated through ancient astrology with the Sun, Moon, and planets, which in turn are associated with the different days of the week. To the ancients, in both East and West, the Sun, Moon, and five known planets were identified as gods, or in Thai parlance, as *thewada*, the Thai word for gods or angels. In this way, too, the names of the days of the week were taken from those of the planet-- gods in both East and some countries of the West – a subject I will come back to later.

What I was able to gather from my wife (and from her friend the astrologer *Achan* Bunchuei) about the "colors of the day" was that these are the colors traditionally associated with the various planet-gods. Thus Sunday's red is the color of the setting sun, and my wife thinks there is also an association with blood (perhaps as a symbol of life, like the Sun). Cream or yellow for Monday is clearly the color of the Moon. Tuesday's god is Mars, and in Thailand (and, I suppose, India, where the Thai tradition presumably came from) Mars is considered to be pink rather than red as in the West.

Wednesday's green is the color associated with Mercury; Thursday's orange or brown, with Jupiter; Friday's blue belongs to Venus; and Saturday's black or purple, of course, to Saturn.

I asked my wife, do rural people still observe this tradition of wearing the correct "color of the day"? No, she replied, but it is now coming back in a different way in the city, purely as a fashion concept or gimmick. (However, she pointed out that Saturday's black is associated with death and is therefore never worn except at funerals; so purple is usually worn on Saturdays, instead).

Moreover, she says that even in the old days, rural people did not know much about these "colors of the day," and consequently did not wear them. It was *khon sung* – the "high-ups" – who knew this tradition and followed it; kings, army commanders-in-chief, generals, and the like.

It was these more learned men who were well versed in astrology. Commanders-in-chief, especially *mae thap*, or "mothers-of-the-army" in Thai, were obliged to know all about astrology. *Achan* Bunchuei filled in the details: it was, he said, necessary for generals and commanders-in-chief to be able to cast their own horoscopes so that they could find out not only the most auspicious day and time to launch the battle, but also the best strategy to conquer their enemies. Part of this strategy was that the commanders must wear the correct "color of the day," depending on which auspicious day had been found for going into battle. The strategy also included certain other ceremonies. The whole strategy, it seems, was designed to instill high morale and courage into the troops – as I pointed out in Chapter 4. *Achan* Bunchuei adds that even today many Thai soldiers learn astrology for more or less the same reason: To be able to examine their own horoscopes so as to find favorable and unfavorable times, and act accordingly.

That seems to be all I can find out about the origins of the "colors of the day." Now for the names of the days of the week in Thai, and in European languages including English.

The same gods or planets in both East and West have been associated with the same corresponding days of the week since time immemorial (or more accurately, since I personally don't know when!). Only the names are different. The Thai names come from Sanskrit, while the European names have come from ancient Rome.

To be more specific, the English names Sunday and Monday come from the Sun and Moon, as do the names of these two days in other European languages. But in English and the other Germanic languages (German, Dutch, the Scandinavian languages) the names of the other days of the week (except Saturday) come from Nordic gods and goddesses. It is in the Latin or "Romance" languages – French, Spanish, and so on – that Tuesday, Wednesday, Thursday, and Friday are named after the Roman planet-gods, the same gods which have given their names to those days in Thai.

On both the Thai and European sides, the close similarities between the modern names and their ancient origins can be clearly seen. Thus *wan athit* is the Thai name for Sunday, *athit* being the Sun; and the Sanskrit origin is *aditya war* (*war*, pronounced to rhyme with "jar," is the Sanskrit for "day"). Similarly, *wan chan* is the Moon's day or Monday in Thai, from the Sanskrit *chandra war*. *Mardi*, the French for Tuesday, comes from Mars, whose day it is. In Thai it is *wan angkhan*, also the day of Mars, from the Sanskrit *mangal war*. Wednesday, *mercredi* or Mercury's day in French, is *wan phut* in Thai, from the Sanskrit *budh war* (nothing to do with the Buddha; *budh* is simply the Sanskrit name for Mercury). *Jeudi*, Jupiter's day or Jove's day, is French for Thursday. In Thai it is *wan pharuehatsabodi*, for short *pharuehat*, from Sanskrit *brahaspati war*, Jupiter's day. Friday in Thai *is wan suk*, Venus' day, from Sanskrit *shukra war*. And in French, Venus' day has become *vendredi*. As for Saturday, the English name obviously means Saturn's day! In Sanskrit it is *shani war*, and in Thai, *wan sao*.

When referring to the actual planets in Thai, the word *dao*, a star, is prefixed. The planet Mars is *dao angkhan*, Mercury is *dao phut*, and so on. The exceptions are the Sun and Moon, known respectively – and respectfully – as *Phra Athit* and *Phra Chan*.

## (2) *Achan* Bunchuei

My wife's astrologer friend *Achan* Bunchuei Chumchueng-rak has been three times President of the Federation of Astrologers. (Perhaps I should explain that the title *Achan* means roughly "teacher," that Bunchuei is his first name, and Chumchuengrak his surname). He was also at one time the Federation's Honorary Secretary. *Achan* Bunchuei is a veteran among Thai astrologers, having been in practice for over thirty years.

I believe it is true to say that in Thailand (and perhaps in Asia generally) astrology is taken a good deal more seriously than in the West. In fact, it has played a vital part in the affairs of the Thai nation ever since its earliest beginnings, and continues to do so today.

Astrology is used in Thailand to find auspicious dates and times of day for almost every imaginable occasion, ranging from the highest state ceremonies to laying the foundation stone of a new hotel or bank, finding out the movements of the stock market, getting married, cutting a child's topknot, or opening a noodle shop.

Like a good many other astrologers in this country, *Achan* Bunchuei was once a soldier. His interest in astrology first began over forty years ago. At that time he was living in Chiang Mai, and had been down on his luck for some time. One day he read an announcement in *The Journal of the Federation of Thai Astrologers* by a successful practicing astrologer, *Achan* Chamrat Siri, about casting horoscopes. He wrote to *Achan* Chamrat, who was then living in Suphan Buri Province, asking him to cast his horoscope. *Achan* Chamrat did so, and found (although Bunchuei had not told him so) that he was going through an unlucky phase of his life. *Achan* Chamrat said it would take another three or four years for the situation to change for the better. It was at this point that Bunchuei's interest in astrology was aroused; he began to wonder how it was that the planets, so far away in the heavens, could have told *Achan* Chamrat that he, Bunchuei, was indeed going through a patch of bad luck.

As predicted, Bunchuei's luck didn't show any signs of picking up. So he got in touch again with *Acham* Chamrat and began learning astrology from him by correspondence. He continued learning doggedly in this way, for several years I suppose, until he had mastered the subject so well that he in turn was able to start teaching it by correspondence himself – which entitled him to become known as *Achan* (teacher) Bunchuei.

There are two recognized astrological organizations in this country (there may be more, for all I know). One of them is the Thai Astrologers' Association, located in the famous royal temple of Wat Bovornnives. *Achan* Bunchuei was at one time secretary of this body, before becoming President of the Federation of Astrologers, as already mentioned, which has its headquarters at another Bangkok temple.

*Achan* Bunchuei sent me a little Thai rhyme about astrology which I have transliterated into the Roman (Western) alphabet and have also translated into English. It ties in with the names of the Sun, Moon, and planets, which are the same as those of the seven days of the week, in both Thai and English or French. Notice that in this rhyme the first seven planets (including the Sun and Moon) are also in the same order as the names of the days of the week; in Thai the word *wan*, meaning "day," is placed in front of the name of each planet. Notice also the special verse form of this rhyme, called a *khloang*: The last word of the second half of each line rhymes with the last word of the first half of the next line. Once again this rhyme shows that Saturn is sometimes a planet of misfortune; as I have already pointed out, Saturday's "color of the day" is black.

Romanized Thai version

| | |
|---|---|
| *Thai yot thai sak* | *hai thai Athit* |
| *Thai chai thai charit* | *hai thai Chan* |
| *Thai kla raeng khaeng khayan* | *hai thai Angkhan* |
| *Thai cheracha on wan* | *hai thai Phut* |
| *Thai panya borisut* | *hai thai Pharuehat* |
| *Thai kilet kamnat* | *hai thai Suk* |
| *Thai thot thai tuk* | *hai thai Sao* |
| *Thai mua mao* | *hai thai Rahu* |
| *Thai ayu yuen yao* | *hai thai Ket* |
| *Thai het aphet* | *hai thai Maruetayu* |

English translation

| TO FIND OUT ABOUT: | LOOK AT: |
|---|---|
| Your status | The Sun |
| Your mannerisms | The Moon |
| Your bravery and diligence | Mars |
| Your silver tongue | Mercury |
| Your wisdom | Jupiter |
| Your desire and lust | Venus |
| Your punishment and woe | Saturn |
| Your wantonness | Rahu (the Earth) |
| Your long life | Ket* |
| Anything strange | Uranus |

## (3) Thai and Western Astrology Compared

People often seem to think that because my wife is an astrologer, I am too. I am not. But as a result I am sometimes asked whether the Thai and Western systems for casting horoscopes are the same, or what differences there are between them.

I asked *Achan* Bunchuei about this and he gave me a written reply in Thai. He says the Thai and Western systems are different. The main difference is that the Western system takes the Sun as its reference point (it is the so-called "movable Zodiac system"), while in the Thai system the Earth is taken as the reference point (the "fixed Zodiac system").

The Western system also has all kinds of auxiliary devices which make it applicable all over the world. The two different viewpoints give apparently different planetary configurations, but in the relationships between the planets there are features common to both systems, and they both give correct predictions. Don't ask me how – as I said, I'm no astrologer!

*Achan* Bunchuei also sent me a little book written and published in India called *Astrology for Beginners*. While reading this, I discovered what I think is a very interesting fact: The Sanskrit names for the twelve signs of the Zodiac bear a close resemblance to the Thai names for the twelve calendar months. The next step was to find out the Thai names for the twelve Zodiac signs, and I found that these are almost identical with the names of the months when written in Thai characters. Because – with all due respect – most Western readers of this book probably cannot read Thai, I have written these names in Roman characters, which means spelling them as they are pronounced rather than as they are written; so the correspondence between the Zodiac sign names and those of the months is not quite so obvious in every case. However, I have put everything in a table:

| Signs of the Zodiac | | | Months | |
|---|---|---|---|---|
| ENGLISH | SANSKRIT | THAI | THAI | ENGLISH |
| Aries | *Mesha* | *Met* | *Mesayon* | April |
| Taurus | *Vrishabha* | *Phreusop* | *Phreusaphakhom* | May |
| Gemini | *Mithuna* | *Mithun* | *Mithunayon* | June |
| Cancer | *Kataka* | *Korakot* | *Karakadakhom* | July |
| Leo | *Simha* | *Sing* | *Singhakhom* | August |
| Virgo | *Kanya* | *Kan* | *Kanyayon* | September |
| Libra | *Tula* | *Tun* | *Tulakhom* | October |
| Scorpio | *Vrischika* | *Phreusachik* | *Phreusachikayon* | November |
| Sagittarius | *Dhanus* | *Thanu* | *Thanwakhom* | December |
| Capricorn | *Makara* | *Makon* | *Makarakhom* | January |
| Aquarius | *Kumbha* | *Kum* | *Kumphaphan* | February |
| Pisces | *Mina* | *Mean* | *Minakhom* | March |

Perhaps the first thing that strikes one about the above table (apart from the similarity between the Thai names for the Zodiac signs and the months) is that the astrologer's year begins with April – just as the old Thai year used to do, with *Songkran* Day being New Year's Day.

I wonder which came first into the Thai language - the names of the Zodiac signs, or those of the months? I have not been able to find out for sure, though I was told that the Zodiac signs are probably older, because astrology has played a vital role in Thai life since ancient times, whereas the calendar months were only introduced comparatively recently. The dates of the signs of the Zodiac follow the months roughly, as you can see by looking at the daily horoscope in your newspaper.

Three of the names in the table are worth commenting on. Cancer is, of course, the Crab, and *Korakot* means a plain ordinary crab in Thai. Leo is the Lion, and *Sing* or *Singha* means "lion" in Thai. And lastly, Sagittarius is the "Archer with his bow and arrow" (*sagitta* is the Latin for "arrow," I remember from my schooldays), and *thanu* means an arrow in Thai.

Finally, my wife has pointed out two differences between astrology and palmistry. Firstly, astrology is concerned with exact dates, days, and times, while palmistry is more general and less precise as far as time is concerned. And secondly, astrology can predict the fortunes of an entire nation – something which palmistry can definitely NOT do!

# CHAPTER NINE
# Names, Words, and Language

## What's in a (Thai) Name?

People's names must surely have as rich a variety in Thailand as anywhere in the world. To begin with, the number of first names (as opposed to surnames) runs into the tens of thousands, and more are being invented almost every day by parents of newborn babies, and by the abbots of local temples who are consulted by parents to whom inspiration about names does not come.

Secondly, nearly every Thai man, woman, and child has a nickname by which they are always known among their family and friends. When you meet someone called "Lek," "Noi," or "Daeng," that is their nickname. "Lek" and "Noi" mean "small" (the owner of the nickname "Lek" may be a huge, hulking giant of a man; but he got the name as a baby, when he was perhaps smaller than average), and "Daeng" means "red."

Thirdly, nearly every Thai name has a meaning. The meaning is almost invariably known to its owner, though it may not be known to anyone else except the owner's mother. And of course, nearly every nickname has a meaning, too; what is the point of having a nickname otherwise?

Let me illustrate these points with my wife and her relatives. There is nothing like starting off with an exception to a rule; so let me say that my wife's real name is Laddawan – a rather common feminine name which means a creeping plant of the convolvulus family with a fragrant flower. She has never had a nickname as such, but her family simply abbreviate her name to "Ladda," or, more usually and economically, "Da." (I have also caught the habit, and at weekends the house rings with my yells of "Da!" when I want something and am too lazy to get out of my chair and fetch it myself. I think I sound rather like a baby who is just learning to talk!)

Ladda's son is always known as "Jiap," but this is only his nickname. It means a baby chick, because when he was small he was very, very small. His real name is Narong, which means "battle"; but Ladda gave him that name for a very special reason. In Thai, "Narong" is spelt without any vowels, and a name without vowels is essential for any child born on a Monday, as Jiap was, to avoid bad luck. This is because the combination of the Moon with the Sun is an evil portent, and the Thai word for the Sun, *athit*, begins with a vowel. So all vowels are associated with the Sun and must be avoided on Monday, which is the "Moon's day."

My wife's sister, Sumalee, has no real nickname either. Her name means "good flower," because the prefix "*su-*," which occurs in a great many Thai names, means "good," and "*malee*" means "a flower." (Not to be confused with the shorter word *mali*, meaning jasmine). Again, my wife usually calls her "Malee" or simply "Lee."

Malee has four children, two boys and two girls. They all have splendid-sounding and unusual names, invented by their mother. The eldest boy is Phongket, which means something like "our family" or "our lineage." The elder girl is Chankhai, "Moon-like"; the younger girl, Chanrawee, "Sun-like"; and the younger boy, Phongsawat, "prosperous family or lineage." But within the family circle and among their friends they are always known by their respective nicknames: Nok, "a bird"; Ap-poen, or Poen for short, the Thai way of pronouncing "Apple"; Khaimuk or Muk, "a pearl"; and Tong, "a large cockerel." It ss hard to say how these nicknames came about; after all, how do Westerners acquire nicknames like "Bud," "Chip," or "Toots"?

Apart from the fact that there are many times more first names in Thailand than in probably any Western country, there is another interesting feature about Thai names: Out of the tens of thousands, there are perhaps two or three hundred which are shared between the sexes, so that it is impossible to tell just from hearing or reading the name whether its owner is male or female.

The remarks and generalizations about Thai names which follow are based on my own experience, and also largely on the book *Phrommachat*, which is full of strange and mysterious Thai folklore. This book lists some 3,700 first names as a guide for parents in naming their children.

Probably the commonest type of Thai first names are compound names with "good," "holy," or "auspicious" meanings. These names often begin or end with words such as *phon*, meaning "blessings," *bun*, "good deeds," *siri or sri* (pronounced "see") meaning "glory," *som* ("fulfillment"), *thong* ("gold"), *thawee* ("to increase"), and other similar words.

For example, the names PENSIRI, PENSRI, SIRIPEN, and SRIPEN all mean "glory of the full moon" – and perhaps needless to say, they are all exclusively female names. But PORNTHAWEE, "increased blessings," can be either male or female, and THAWEESAK, "increased status," is a man's name. (It can be spelt in the Western alphabet in four or five different ways according to the taste of the owner). THONGSUK, "sheen of gold," is usually a man's name.

Two "good" words are often joined together to form such frequently-seen names as SOMBOON and BOONSOM, "good deeds fulfilled"; SIRIBOON and BOONSIRI; PORNSRI and SIRIPORN; and so on. Most of these "good" names belong equally to both sexes.

Among other fairly common names which can be either male or female are AMPHON, "the sky," and UTHAI and AROON, both of which mean "dawn." (UTHAI is met in Thailand's ancient capital of Sukhothai, which means "the dawn of happiness," while most visitors will be familiar with AROON or ARUN through the Temple of Dawn, Wat Arun). Then there are AREE, "compassionate"; SAMRONG, "understudy"; SUPARB, "polite"; BANG-ERN, "unexpected"; SOMWANG, "hope fulfilled"; BOONCHU, "supported by good deeds"; and WATFANA and PATFANA, both of which mean "progress." All these and many more are the names of men and women, in roughly equal numbers I suppose. SUPORN can also be either a man's or woman's name; and PORN means "blessing." so SUPORN means "good blessings."

Readers will in all probability have met at least one Thai whose name begins with SU. I will just give one or two examples here: SUPHOT, exclusively a man's name, meaning "good words," and SUWILAI, which means "good as well as beautiful" because WILAI (sometimes spelt VILAI) means "beautiful" – and which, I hardly need add, is exclusively a lady's name!

Now, two or three hundred names which may be either male or female may seem quite a lot, especially to Westerners most of whose native tongues do not have ANY such names at all. (There are no names in English which are identical for both men and women as far as I know; the possible exception is SYDNEY. LESLIE is a man's name; the feminine form is spelt LESLEY.)

But in the vast ocean of Thai names, two or three hundred names shared between the sexes is a mere drop. In Thailand, as in most other countries in the world, the great majority of names are reserved exclusively for one or other of the sexes. And as might be expected, the meanings of most men's names tend to emphasize strong, masculine qualities, while women's names are concerned with soft, feminine virtues.

So among men's names we find meanings such as "bold," "famous," "dragon," "steadfast" (which is DAMRONG), "proud." Other men's names have milder but nevertheless honorable-sounding meanings such as "peace" (SANTI), "permanent" (THAVORN or TAWORN), "helpful," "silver," "clever," "history," and "son of the Buddha."

Two particularly common endings for men's names are CHAI, which may mean either "male" or "victory," according to how it is spelt in Thai, but usually means the latter (SOMCHAI may be spelt either way, meaning respectively "manly" or "victory fulfilled"); and SAK, sometimes spelt SAKDI (the -DI is silent), which means "prestige" or "status," of which examples abound: CHOOSAK, SOMSAK, TERMSAK, TAWEESAK, and many more.

The meanings of those last two names, TERMSAK and THAWEESAK, are interesting illustrations of the extreme subtlety of Thai names. TERMSAK means "added status" in the sense that one adds sugar or salt where there was none before; THAWEESAK means "increased status." Some Thais might argue that the difference is even less clear-cut than this!

Most women's names in Thailand, as in other countries, emphasise beauty and other good feminine qualities, or are names of flowers, plants, or fruits. Two rather rare women's names which I find especially charming are JANPHET, "moon diamond," and CHULIKON, meaning to *wai* or make the universal Thai greeting of respect. Common endings for women's names are -JIT, meaning "mind," and -JAI, "heart." SOMJAI, "getting one's heart's desire," can belong to either sex, but is mostly a feminine name.

The meaning of "angel" or "angelic" occurs in men's names, mainly as the suffix -THEP, (as in Bangkok's Thai name, KRUNG THEP, the City of Angels), giving such common names as SUTHEP and PORNTHEP. A similar-sounding word, TIP, occurs in women's names: It means "magic". So there is PORNTIP, "magic blessings"; TIPMANEE, "magic jewel"; and NAMTIP, "magical drink". (In these examples, TIP may also be spelt THIP, according to choice.)

Two other men's names with "good" meanings which come to my mind are SA-ART, "clean," and PRADIT, "invent."

You may often see WAN as the beginning or ending of a Thai name, and this may be a very deep and ancient word. It all depends on the Thai spelling; I know three ways of spelling WAN, and there may be others. In the man's name WANCHAI, WAN simply means "day," so this name means "day of victory." In my wife's name LADDAWAN, it is part of the whole name of the fragrant creeping plant.

But in its Sanskrit form, WAN contains no vowels in the Thai spelling; it is written WRRN. This form has many meanings: "complexion," "kind of," "sex," "book," "class or caste," "gold," "beautiful," "celebrity," and "pure or white." This Sanskrit form usually appears at the end of feminine names such as BENJAWAN, "of five kinds," SIRIWAN, "pure glory," and KAMOLWAN, "pure heart."

That last name, KAMOLWAN, when written in Thai, contains no vowels at all; it is spelt GMLWRRN. It belongs to the class of vowel-less names which, as I mentioned earlier, must always be given to a child born on a Monday. Other names in this class are GORAGOT, spelt GRGT, the Zodiac sign of the Crab; NOPPADON, spelt NPDL, "the sky"; and my stepson's name, NARONG, spelt NRNGK, "battle."

Now for some more details about nicknames. These are much more universal than in the West; everybody in Thailand seems to have one. Sometimes they are just shortened forms of the person's real name, as in the West; but usually they bear no resemblance to it.

The commonest nicknames mean "small": LEK, NIT, NOI, TOI. This has nothing to do with the person's present physical size; these nicknames were given as terms of endearment when their owners were babies. DAENG, "red," is also common; I know at least four in our office – three women and a man. Another common girl's nickname is OY, "sweet" or literally "sugarcane." The other day I heard of a thin, rather skinny boy whose nickname is CHANG – "elephant"!

Other nicknames – none of them the slightest bit derogatory – are GOONG, "shrimp"; MAEO, "cat"; MOO, "pig"; and "GOI," "little finger".

Nicknames are sometimes given by parents who want their offspring to grow up sturdy and healthy. One such is TUME (it rhymes with "room"), which means "a pendulum." This expresses the wish that the person will become plump and round, like the bob of a pendulum!

All in all, Thai names are indeed almost a microcosm of Thai attitudes and culture. And the same is true of Thai surnames, which are dealt with in the next section.

## Surnames

An English professor on an official visit to this country was invited by a Thai colleague, whom I will call Professor Sophon, to the latter's house to meet his wife and family. The Englishman had only been in Thailand a few days and did not know much about Thai customs. On being introduced to the Thai professor's wife, he innocently said "How do you do, Mrs. Sophon?"

A perfectly natural mistake, and one which must surely have been made by many other foreign visitors to Thailand. In fact, the lady's name was not Mrs. Sophon at all; it happened to be Mrs. Vimolwan. As all visitors to this country discover sooner or later, Thais are invariably known in conversation by their first names – even when the name is preceded by "Professor." "Dr.," "Mrs.," and so on.

Thai surnames are NEVER used on their own, in the way Westerners refer to "Professor Smith," "Mr. Brown," or "Mrs. Jones." Not even in the telephone directory. If you glance through the English version of the directory, you will see that all personal entries (as opposed to companies and so on) are listed alphabetically under the person's FIRST name.

In the anecdote above, the Englishman had originally been introduced to Professor Sophon by someone else, and had assumed without question that "Sophon" was the man's surname. If he had seen the professor's full name spelled out on a name card, he might well have blanched on reading his actual surname, which was quite long and at first glance almost totally unpronounceable!

In spoken Thai, surnames are added after the first name only in formal speech (such as in radio or television announcements) and even then, only the first time the person is mentioned; all further references to that person use the first name alone. The same rule is followed in the local press, both Thai and English-language. The only exception to this rule is when one is talking (or writing) about two people who both have the same first name; the surnames of both must be added, to avoid confusion.

(Even this is not always one hundred per cent successful. When my stepson Narong was working in his first job, there was another Narong in the same department. So whenever my wife rang him up, she had to ask for Narong Piamchan. Unfortunately the other Narong's surname was Piam-charoen, which sounds very nearly the same, and as often as not the wrong Narong came to the phone!)

The first-name habit is so deeply ingrained in Thai society that sometimes Thais who have known each other for years do not know each other's surnames. And there is a very simple reason for this. It was only in 1913 that surnames were introduced into Thailand. Before that, they were completely unknown anywhere in the kingdom, and the only way of identifying someone was by referring to him as the son of Mr. "X," or as hailing from "Y" village. (Alter all, that is exactly how many English surnames originated – Johnson, McDonald, O'Leary, Stirling, and so on.)

In 1913 King Vajiravudh (Rama VI) introduced surnames to Thailand in order to make social life easier and better for everyone, rich and poor alike. He personally invented surnames for families of high rank, as well as for many other families who petitioned him to do so. In each case he specified the precise spelling of the surname, not only in Thai, but also in Roman (Western) characters. He also took steps to ensure that no two unrelated families in the land ever had the same surname. This remains the case, with very few exceptions, today.

I mentioned in the last section that every one of the tens of thousands of Thai first names has a meaning, although as often as not the meaning may be known only to its owner and his or her mother. The same applies to surnames: Every Thai surname has a meaning, although it may or may not be obvious to everyone. To take the first example that comes to my mind, the surname "Meesuk" means "happy," and this is obvious to every Thai. On the other hand, neither my wife nor her son Narong knows the meaning of his surname "Piamchan." A friend of mine says it might mean "full class" or "full rank," whatever that means!

In fact there does seem to be a certain vagueness about some people's surnames, especially in the rural areas. My wife's maiden name was "Aroonchol," which means "the morning tide." But her father's surname had a "J" on the front- it was "Jaroonchol" (actually the spellings of the two names are different in Thai) – and in the process of registering her birth at the local *amphoe*, or district office, somehow or other the name was mistakenly entered as "Aroonchol." A few years ago, pondering on the fact that all her relatives were called "Jaroonchol" and she was the only one with the wrong spelling, she went to the district office and got her surname changed back again to "Jaroonchol."

But in some mysterious Thai way beyond my grasp, my wife's sister acquired her grandmother's surname, which was "Tongpanchiwa." This has a rather deep and romantic-sounding meaning – something like "golden as life itself."

When King Vajiravudh issued his Royal Edict that every person in the kingdom must have a surname, and himself invented many surnames, he leaned towards the Sanskrit spelling, in both the Thai and Romanized forms. The possession of these royally conferred surnames was, of course, regarded as a great honor by the families concerned, and

214

still is by their descendants. Most of these descendants have kept to the original spelling – which is one reason why that Englishman might have found Professor Sophon's surname so difficult to pronounce.

As for the effect of the Royal Edict on rural village families, some rather interesting things happened. One delightful story, unconfirmed but well worth repeating all the same, concerns what took place in a small country village when the royal command reached it.

All the villagers assembled under the huge tamarind tree which served as the village meeting place, and put their heads together. But inspiration did not come; no one could think of any surnames.

Finally one man, glancing up at the tree above them, said, "Very well, I will call my family Tamarind-leaf (*bai-makham*)."

Immediately, another spoke up: "In that case, I will call mine Tamarind-branch (king-makham)." A third said, "Right – mine's Tamarind-seed (met-makham)." In this way every part of the tree – bark, trunk, roots, and soon-was called into use as a family name, and all these "Tamarind" surnames are said to have survived to this day.

Another surname, "Saengbangpla," was made up from the grandfather's first name, Saeng, meaning "light," and the village from which the family came, Bang Pla or Fish Village in Samut Prakarn province.

A friend of mine has another interesting surname, "Sonsomsook." This was a case of simple addition: a man named "Son" married a lady called "Som" and they had a son called "Sook." What could be simpler? With surnames being invented or evolving in ways such as these, it is easy to understand why – like Thai first names – every Thai surname has a meaning.

Readers who watch Thai television may have heard this little joke about surnames, which was told to me by a Thai colleague. "You lazy good-for-nothing!" The angry father scolded his son. "Why must you spend all your time loafing around the house? Why don't you remember our family's proud surname – 'Rak-ngan' ("love work")?"

"I didn't choose our surname, Dad," retorted the youth, stifling a yawn. "If I had, I wouldn't have chosen 'Rak-ngan' – I would have chosen 'Rak-non' ('love sleeping')!"

## The World's Longest Place-Name

Not only personal names and surnames but also many place-names in Thailand have meanings. Here is one you may have heard of: "City of Angels, great city of immortals, magnificent jeweled city of the god Indra, seat of the King of Ayutthaya, city of gleaming temples, city of the King's most excellent Palace and Dominions, home of Vishnu and all the gods."

In other words, Bangkok.

In Thai, it is all joined into one vast word of 160 letters:

*Krungthepmahanakhonamonrattanakosin*
*mahintharaayutthayamahadilokphopnopharat*
*rathaniburiromudomrachainwetmahasathan*
*amonphimanavatansathitsakkattiyavisanukamprasit.*

No wonder the Guinness Book of Records lists it as the world's longest place-name. It makes that place in Wales with the longest railway station signboard in Britain, Llanfairpwll-something-or-other, look pretty silly. It has only got fifty-eight letters. Ridiculously small.

Bangkok was not always known by this magnificent name. Before it became Thailand's capital in 1782, it was only a small village by the Chao Phya River, and was just called . . . Bangkok. Or, more accurately, "Bang Makok."

"Bang" means a riverside village, and "Makok" is an olive or a kind of plum. (The shortened form "Bangkok," used universally by foreigners, still survives in Thai in the names of two canals on the Thonburi side of the river – *Khlong* Bangkok Yai and *Khlong* Bangkok Noi).

Across the river, Thonburi means "city of wealth," a reminder that it was founded by King Taksin, whose name also implies riches. And the correct name of the river itself is Mae Nam Chao Phya, or "Most noble mother of waters."

The meanings of Thailand's place-names are full of rich historic interest and color. Even in the Metropolis, districts and street names have meanings, which as foreigners we are not always aware of.

Do you live in Shrimp-paste Village? It is one of the most fashionable residential areas of Bangkok. Perhaps you know it better by its Thai name: Bangkapi. Or you may be more centrally situated in Enjoyment Road or one of the lanes leading off it, such as Pine Tree Lane or the Lane at the Back of the Garden. In other words, Ploenchit Road, Soi Ton Son, or Soi Lang Suan. If so, you are conveniently near the shopping areas of Inside-the-Flower Road, or the Roads of Royal Purpose, Royal Opinion or Royal Remark. In case you are not sure which they are, you will know them better as Gayson, Rajprasong, Rajdamri, and Rajprarop respectively.

Perhaps you work in the busy commercial district of Windmill Road, or maybe in the older Prosperous City Road. In Thai, they are known as Silom and Charoen Krung, or New Road.

And what about Red Earth Road and Buffalo Bridge? (Din

217

Daeng Road and Saphan Khwai; the latter probably got its name from the days when buffaloes were brought to the city from the provinces by boat; they disembarked from a canal near this point and crossed over a bridge where the crossroad now stands.) Bangkok's airport is also rather aptly named: The City's High Ground, or in Thai, Don Muang.

Three royal highways lead out of Bangkok: The Road of the Army of Warriors going north (Phaholyothin); the Road of Wisdom, or Sukhumvit, going southeast; and the Road of Diamond Happiness (Phetkasem) going west and south. Heading north, let us wander off the highway and visit the Town of Happiness and Lotus Town. As their names imply, Nonthaburi and Pathum Thani are both pleasant places.

Further on we will come to the Village Where I Met the Girl Called In, or Bang Pa-In. And so to Pond Town, or Saraburi. ("Buri" means "town" in Thai, of course, just as "bury" or "borough" do in English – and for a very good and ancient reason: They both come from a common ancestor-word in the Indo-European language, five thousand years ago). Gold deposits are said to have been found at one time in the province of that name – Gold Town, or Suphan Buri. From this gold perhaps the Golden Bowl was made which gives nearby Ang Thong its name.

Not far away is Singapore – or rather, a variation of the same name, which means Lion Town: Sing Buri. Things begin to look up as we pass Victorious Cheer or Chainat, skirting Sunrise Town or Uthai Thani on our left, for soon we arrive at the Heavenly City, Nakhon Sawan.

Leaving the Warriors' Highway for a while, we take a right fork and visit such historic towns as the World of the God Vishnu and the Dawn of Happiness, once the capital of a powerful kingdom. The Thai names for these towns are Phitsanulok and Sukhothai.

Nearby is another Heavenly World, well known for its pottery – Sawankhalok. Further on is the town whose name means "Well-Known,": Phrae; and near the Lao border we come to the town aptly named Boundary, or Nan.

Coming back again onto the Warriors' Highway, we will meet another historic city with a sparkling name – the Diamond Wall, or Kamphaeng Phet. A little bit further north is a town whose name means "Exposed to the Sun," Tak.

The capital in the north, dating from the thirteenth century, was originally known as "the New City" – and still is. In Thai, its name is Chiang Mai.

## Some Sayings and Proverbs

*"Phut pai song phai bia,*
*Ning sia tamlueng thong."*

That old Thai saying, translated literally, means "Speak out – two *phai bia* (old Thai coins of extremely low value); keep quiet – a gold *tamlueng* (an old coin worth four baht)." Remembering that a baht was quite a sizeable sum of money in olden times when that saying first came into use, we can see that the meaning is the same as that of the equally old English saying, "Speech is silver; silence is golden."

This is just one of about eight hundred Thai proverbs and sayings in a tattered old book I have at home. I do not know how I acquired it or where it came from; I just know I have it. The book is called *Suphasit Khamphangpheoi Khamkhom*, or "Sayings, proverbs, and witticisms."

It is a real treasure-house of Thai folklore. As is often done in English compilations of proverbs, the meanings of many of the proverbs are explained in the book. If only (sigh) I had a completely bilingual Thai translator with unlimited free time (and patience) and a strong sense of humour, sitting beside me for say three or four days, the things I could get out of that book!

These proverbs provide yet another perspective on Thai culture which I find completely fascinating. The expressions used reflect Thailand's agricultural traditions; how much nicer is "Taking coconuts to sell in the orchard" than industrial Britain's mucky, murky "Taking coals to Newcastle"!

Actually I was quite lucky, because a Thai friend who is bilingual did spend most of a quiet and pleasant (and rather hot) Sunday afternoon with me, trying to find the nearest English equivalents for some of the proverbs in the book. We did not get through nearly as many as I would have liked, because as often as not the corresponding English proverb would be on the tips of our tongues, but somehow we just could not nail it down.

"Mistaking the rim of a wheel for a lotus flower." That suggests taking something to be much superior to what it really is, or as the English proverb has it, "Trying to make a silk purse out of a sow's ear." And while we are on the subject of pigs, how about "Offering a jewel to an ape?" Yes, I am concentrating on what I am writing; that proverb is obviously the same as "Casting pearls before swine"!

"Ten cowrie shells near the hand." Several knowledgeable Thai friends, including my Sunday-afternoon helper, all seem quite sure that means "a bird in the hand is worth two in the bush." (Come to think of it, many of our English proverbs seem to have an agricultural bias, too.)

"Red ants guarding a cluster of mangoes" does not seem to mean very much unless you happen to know that red ants are not particularly fond of mangoes. But given that fact, "a dog in the manger" conveys the exact meaning. The book also gives two other proverbs having the same meaning; one of them is word for word the same as in English, while the other is "a dog jealously guarding a fishbone."

One saying which I particularly like is "talking like water flowing enough to put out a fire" – or as we say it in English, "talking nineteen to the dozen"!

Some other sayings and proverbs in the book which are very similar or even identical to their English counterparts, are "Draw a picture of a tiger to frighten a cow," which seems to mean the same as the saying we have taken from China, "a paper tiger"; "if you already have a dog, don't bark yourself" – that one barks (I mean speaks) for itself! "Still waters run deep" and "don't get ideas above your station" are both word for word the same in Thai and English.

There is another English proverb with more or less the same meaning as that last one: "Cut your coat according to your cloth." The book gives three proverbs all of which seem to fit that one; "comb your hair to suit your face; buy cloth to suit your status," "small birds build nests just the right size for them," and "if you only have a little, use it slowly and carefully." (Just what it is that you must only a use little of, is not specified: Toothpaste, perhaps?)

Other proverbs and sayings in the book were a bit more difficult to find English equivalents for. "Pushing a heavy mortar uphill." After some hesitation we decided on "swimming against the current" as the nearest we could find. "The water goes down, then rises again." Now, what on earth could that mean? The explanation given in the book seems to suggest "bad deeds, like chickens, come home to roost."

Some rather more obvious ones gave us a lot of fun. How

about "riding an elephant to catch a grasshopper"? That seems to mean exactly the same as "using a sledgehammer to crack a nut"! Another, which uses a double metaphor to drive home its point, is "a chicken is beautiful because of its feathers; people are made beautiful by their clothes." That is easy, we said to each other – "fine feathers make fine birds." Another double-metaphor proverb in the book is "love a cow, keep it tied up; love a child, beat him." "Spare the rod, spoil the child," is it not?

"Don't cut the bamboo stem (to make a water container) before you see the water; don't draw your bow before you see the squirrel." Or as we would say in English, don't count your chickens before they are hatched.

"If there is fire inside, don't take it outside; if there is fire outside, don't bring it inside," another one runs. This idea of not spreading something bad is probably best rendered by our saying "don't wash your dirty linen in public." (There is also, incidentally, a shorter and more salty Thai proverb with the same meaning – "don't pull out your intestines to feed to the crows"!)

"When inspecting an elephant, examine its tail; when inspecting a (prospective) bride, examine her mother!" The nearest English expression we could find for that was "like father, like son." And "step over a fallen tree-trunk; don't step over a fallen person" is surely "don't hit a man when he's down."

The book also devotes a complete chapter to what it calls "comparison phrases" (like the English "as fit as a fiddle"). Here are a few taken at random.

"As industrious as a crow" seems to be the same as "as busy as a bee." "As white as a tuft of cotton (on the cotton plant)" is what English speakers would call "as white as snow" (brr-r-r! Give me the tuft of cotton any day).

"As quiet as blowing on a pestle" (which normally makes a lot of noise when used for pounding rice); well, I suppose "as quiet as a mouse" fits well enough. There is also "to talk like a meandering river," which might perhaps mean the same as "beating about the bush." And in Thailand, it is "as fat as a water jar" – not a pig!

But what about the rather poetic expression "to wait as a rice plant waits for rain"? Does that mean the same as "with the patience of a saint"?

Some other interesting proverbs from the book are given below. I have made them into a quiz; readers may enjoy trying to find the corresponding English proverbs. Most of them are quite easy, and matching them is fun. (Answers are given at the end of this section.)

1. Escape from a tiger, and meet a crocodile.
2. Don't get worried before you have a fever.
3. Teaching the Supreme Patriarch to read and write. (No prizes for that!)
4. If the dancing's bad, blame the flute and the drums. (Or that!)
5. When the water rises, hurry to collect some.
6. When you visit the country where they blink their eyes, you must blink your eyes too!
7. When the cow's gone, surround the cattle-pen.
8. Some like meat, others prefer medicine.
9. After you've been hurt, you will remember it.
10. Losing a little is difficult; losing a lot is easy.
11. (Same meaning as no. 10) Something tiny escapes an elephant's eye; something huge escapes a mite's eye.
12. Applying gold leaf to the back of a Buddha image. (Where one isn't noticed; most people do it more obviously, on the front.)
13. To get something, one must sacrifice something.

14. Cast a spell on the ladle, and your husband will love you until his dying day.
15. To dive down a cobra's throat.

Now, here is one which does not mean what you might think: "Like flood-water on a duck's back." That does NOT mean "like water off a duck's back"! The meaning is simply "impossible" – because no matter how hard it tries, a duck cannot sink beneath the surface of water!

There are many proverbs in the book which proved beyond our powers of matching. For instance, there are three sayings which all have the meaning of doing something useless: "Playing the flute to a buffalo," "giving spectacles to a blind man," and "giving a bald-headed man a comb."

Other teasers are "great greed will cause benefits to disappear" (killing the golden goose?); "slapping someone on the head (a great insult), then stroking him consolingly on the back"; "catching a fish with both hands" (wearing a belt and braces, perhaps?); "breaking a shaft across one's knee"; "covering a dead elephant with a lotus leaf"; "write with the hand, rub out with the foot"; "pounding milled rice, then pouring it into a pot"; and "even a four-legged animal can stumble, and so can a philosopher."

Somehow I have the feeling that there are English proverbs lurking around with exactly the same meanings, but I just cannot put my finger on them.

Another Thai saying which is totally untranslateable is *"chut tai tam to,"* or "light a torch, but still trip over the tree-stumps." This means being placed in an unexpectedly embarrassing position – such as telling someone in a strange town that you do not think much of the local mayor, and then finding it is the mayor himself you are talking to!

There is one very common English saying which almost certainly originated in Thailand: "A white elephant." White elephants are very much prized in this country, but they are also very expensive to keep. It is said that Siamese kings of old who wanted to bring financial ruin on an adversary in order to conquer him, would make him a present of a white elephant!


## ANSWERS TO PROVERBS QUIZ

1. Out of the frying pan into the fire.
2. Don't meet your troubles half-way.
3. Teaching your grandmother to suck eggs.
4. A bad workman blames his tools.
5. Make hay while the sun shines (or, strike while the iron's hot).
6. When in Rome, do as the Romans do.
7. Shutting the stable door after the horse has gone.
8. One man's meat is another man's poison.
9. Once bitten, twice shy (or, a burnt child dreads the fire).
10. and 11. Penny wise, pound foolish.
12. Doing good by stealth.
13. You can't make an omelette without breaking eggs.
14. The way to a man's heart is through his stomach.
15. Putting one's head in the lion's mouth.

# The Versatile Thai "Child"

One of my most useful sources of information is the *New Model Thai-English Dictionary*, and its companion volume, the *New Model English-Thai Dictionary*, both of them compiled by So Sethaputra (pronounced "Sor Settaboot"). My copy of *the Thai-English Dictionary* was printed in 1971, and of the English-Thai, in 1970. (There are probably later editions of these dictionaries, which are published by Thai Watana Panich.)

"The dictionary . . . gives a fairly comprehensive picture of Thailand – its more important place-names, its institutions, literature, and drama, as well as its religious background," writes the compiler in his foreword. This is certainly true; I, for one, find it fascinating reading. Although I am in no way an expert in linguistics or language, I believe that the language of a country can tell a lot about the attitude of its people towards life in general. The details of a nation's attitude to life cannot be put into words – at least, they are too subtle for me to do so; but this dictionary, particularly the Thai-English volume, helps to convey the feel, the flavor, the very essence of Thailand.

A good example is the prolific Thai word *luk*, meaning a child. The syllable is long, as in the English word "fluke," and the tone is a falling one, surprised-sounding, as one might say in English slang, "Coo! Just fancy that!"

On its own, *luk* has only a few meanings: A child; a ball; a bag; and as a "classifier" (a noun used for saying how many of a thing there are) for fruit, balls, and typhoons. For instance: *kluai sam luk* – three bananas; *luk tennit sam luk* – three tennis balls; and *taifun sam luk* – three typhoons.

But it is the wealth of compound words formed by joining another word onto the end of *luk* which I find so interesting. There are 131 of them in So Sethaputra's dictionary. The dictionary says: *Luk* – the first element in many compounds meaning a minor, a subordinate, the object of an action or the complement of a thing . . . sometimes equivalent to the English suffix "-ee," as *luk-chang*, "employee."

Among these *luk-* compounds are words with meanings one would expect, such as "son." "daughter," "lamb," "calf,"and the young of other animals. Then there are a few words of the kind mentioned above, with the meaning of "minions, hirelings, underlings": *Luk-kalo, luk-nong, luk-laeng, luk-samun, luk-chok.*

But what does "the complement of a thing" mean? Well, I suppose one example is *luk-peun*, "child of a gun" – that is, a bullet (not "son-of-a-gun"). Another example in the same category is *luk-kit*, "child of counting" – that is, an abacus! And again, *luk-fai*, "child of fire" – sparks!

Other interesting *luk-* compounds are *luk-krok*, "the offspring of a slave," a reminder that slavery was abolished in this country only as recently as 1905; *luk-krok* and *luk-pla* also mean "fingerlings," and *luk-pla* has another meaning – "small round pieces of paper for pasting on a kite."

"Fingerlings"... What on earth are they? I looked them up in the *Concise Oxford Dictionary*; all it said was "Fingerlings: Parr." Parr? Was that the name of one of Henry the Eighth's wives? So I looked up "parr," and found it meant "young salmon." Of course! *luk pla* – "child of a fish"!

*Luk-krok* – "a stillborn offspring, especially of a cat, believed to bring good luck," says So Sethaputra. Chancing to mention this word to my wife reminded her that when she was small she once found such a stillborn kitten, no bigger that her little finger, among a litter of kittens which one of her grandmother's cats had just produced. Her grandmother was away at the time, spending the night at the temple, and my wife threw the tiny thing away. On her return her grandmother scolded her for not keeping it in a box; it would have made all the family rich, she said.

My wife went on to say that stillborn puppies and even premature stillborn human babies are cherished upcountry in the same way even today, and for the same reason. A human foetus of this type is kept on a solid gold or silver pedestal, or *phan*, and offerings of rice are placed before it daily.

Here are some other interesting meanings of *luk-* words given in So Sethaputra's dictionary: A tadpole; balustrades; the Adam's apple; a roller (for the lawn, or for a printing press or other machinery); candy; a spinning-top; a jury, or jurors; a clucking sound from the throat; a subcontractor; a kind of vegetable dye; "child of a chain," in other words, a link in a chain; and "child of a flower." No, if you think that is pollen, you are wrong-it means a dart or game of darts!

Also in the list are buttons; a porcelain insulator; the rank and file; stakes driven into a tree for easy climbing; bamboo rafts used as pontoons for floating heavy logs; cube, cubic meter and so on; a doorknob; and "child of a boat," or the boat crew!

There are also a pulley, block, tackle, bomb, grenade, a wheel, a piston; a toy balloon; the fruit of the snuffbox bean; a kneecap; a boy scout; encouragement or backing; a kind of firework; the finale of a musical composition; marbles; moth-balls; and a babe in arms. Not forgetting, perhaps, one of the commonest of all – *luk-kha*, "a child of trade" – a customer or client.

Returning to that expression in the dictionary, "the complement of a thing," the word for a key is *luk-kunchae*. If the key is the child, then what is the lock?

Well, of course, the mother! A lock is *mae-kunchae*.

So let us leave all those motley *luk-* words and see what *mae-*, "mother-," has to offer.

There are not nearly as many words, but here are some interesting ones; *mae-ngan*, "mother of work," or chief; *mae-thap*, "mother of an army," or commander-in-chief; *mae-raeng*, "a strong mother" – a jack for lifting a car! *Mae-si*, "mother-colors," that is, primary colors; *mae-lek*. "mother of iron" . . . Care to guess? A magnet!

But perhaps the best known of all such *mae-* words to us foreigners is "mother of water" – *mae-nam*, a river.


## Words Ancient and Modern

When I first came to Thailand in 1965, a kind friend started teaching me the rudiments of the Thai language. One of the most basic words in any language is "I," and my friend taught me the Thai word for this, which she said was *"chan."*

Like a conscientious student I wrote down everything she told me in a notebook, and I was a bit hesitant whether to write that word as *chan* or *chun*: However carefully I listened, the sound seemed to be halfway between the two – as indeed it is. Moreover, every time my friend uttered that word *chan*, I couldn't help noticing the rising inflection in her voice – almost as if she were asking a question.

It was a year or more before I began to realise the subtleties of Thai tones, the precise way in which they are indicated in Thai script, and their essential importance for the meaning of a word. For instance, *chan* in an ordinary tone means "upright," while *chan* in a high tone means a floor or storey of a building, or a class (in schools, railway stations and so on).

But I am digressing. The point I want to make concerns another kind of subtlety, to do with social customs and politeness. Alter I had picked up a smattering of Thai, a colleague heard me referring to myself as *chan* when talking to an equal. "You shouldn't say *chan*," she told me in English. "When a man addresses an equal or a superior, the word he should use for "I" is not *chan*, but *phom*.* A man should only use *chan* when he is addressing an inferior." She went on to add that *phom* also means "the hair on one's head."

Later I learnt that a woman uses *chan* when speaking to equals or inferiors alike; she uses a more polite form, *dichan*, only on special occasions, such as when talking to a stranger who is obviously her equal or superior.

Over the years I gradually grew into the habit of referring to myself as *phom* to almost everyone – superiors, equals and inferiors, just to be on the safe side. (I'm just beginning to train myself to say *chan* when talking to children.)

*Phom*, like *chan*, also has a rising, questioning tone. Only quite recently did I begin wondering why this word, which means "hair of the head" for both sexes, is also used by males to mean "I."

I asked one or two Thai friends. One of them said, "I would need to do a bit of research to give you an answer." Another said simply, "Goodness, I have no idea!" A third said, "They are two different words, which happen to be spelt and pronounced the same. One word means 'hair,' the other means 'I'."

Yet it is strange the way apparently quite unimportant occurrences or casual remarks sometimes link up with other ideas in one's mind. I had already intended to devote some space to quoting the late Mom Rachawong Ayumongol Sonakul's former column "Soliloquies," concerning what I

*This was originally spelled "*pom*" by the authot (Ed.).

230

wrote about *phom* meaning "I" and *phom* meaning "hair." Then my wife said something quite by chance which I believe goes a little bit further towards completing the picture.

My wife had been cutting my hair. Nowadays she does this regularly; I have not been to a barber for years. She had cut it, as always, on our verandah with me sitting upright in an ordinary chair, a towel wrapped round me. (She cuts it quite well, although sometimes when it is finished she stands back and has a hearty laugh at the somewhat surrealistic results of her scissor-work!)

I stood up, removed the towel and shook the hair trimmings onto the floor. Then my wife said, "*Ham yiap phom*," which means "you mustn't step on the hair" (the trimmings on the floor). Immediately I understood – and echoes of M.R. Ayumongol's column raced through my mind. "The hair is the most exalted part of the body, and the foot is the lowest," my wife added. It might almost have been M.R. Ayumongol himself speaking. My wife continued, "because the hair is high, to step on it with the lowest part of the body is an insult. Upcountry, this is believed to bring bad luck and deprive one of one's personal power."

For the same reason, or a similar reason, she said, there are good and bad days for cutting hair. And, as I have pointed out earlier, Wednesday is the one day in the week on which one must NEVER cut hair in Thailand. (Nor one's nails either.) But my wife has no idea why Wednesday has such a bad effect on hair.

Anyway, to get back to the main topic – the connection between *phom* meaning "I" and *phom* meaning "hair."

I am reproducing the relevant parts of M.R. Ayumongol's column below, because I found them so extremely interesting, and I feel sure readers will, too. I would like to say a very warm "thank you" to him for helping to make the picture of the Thai way of saying "I" (or avoiding saying it) more complete.

Here are the relevant extracts from the column.

Let us move on to Denis Segaller's "Thai Ways." I am writing this because my mother read his last offering and got *tok rong* (there, now, is another Thai expression for Mr. Segaller to research). She wants me to write about it, and I know I shall never get any peace until I do.

My mother's obsession (a clue there, Mr. Segaller: But find the etymology yourself!) concerns Mr. Segaller's explanation of the word *phom*, meaning "I" or "hair."

Mr. Segaller uses the transliteration *pom*. Actually, I would prefer *phom* myself since *pom* looks like Australian for an Englishman.

Anyway, Mr. Segaller says he could discover no connection between the two meanings. Nor could his Thai friends, some of whom said "don't know," while others said "no connection."

The two meanings are indeed the same: "hair," not "I."

To understand this, you must first know that there is no one specific word for "I" in contemporary Thai. You can get into all sorts of weird constructions to convey it, or even build your sentences so as to leave it out entirely. The same difficulty occurs with "you."

When you are referring to yourself as *phom* (or *pom*, if Mr. Segaller insists), you are saying not "I" but "my hair."

This comes from the old custom of using a high part of your anatomy to address a lower part of the anatomy of a higher personage. For example an untitled commoner would call himself *phom* when addressing a commoner with the title of *Phya*, whom he would address as *tai thao* (sole of the feet). *"Phom rian tai thao"* – literally, "my hair is addressing the soles of your feet." Similarly, when talking to a prince, you would call yourself *kramom* (or *gramorm*, in Mr. Segaller's transliteration), and call the prince *fa bat*, literally: "The top of my head is addressing the soles of your royal feet."

I do not blame Mr. Segaller for not knowing this. Many Thais do not, either. There used to be a man at Hua Hin who used to call himself *fa baht* when talking to a prince because by his reasoning he was lowly and should be represented by the lowest part of the body. He did not understand the subtlety of the language. My mother got *tok rong* about his wrong usage too, and spent years trying to educate him – happily, I am glad to say, with no result: Three cheers for his victory!

Incidentally, the use of *phom* to refer to oneself when talking to an equal is relatively new. The standard form for "I" when talking to equals used to be *chan*, which was mentioned by Mr. Segaller and definitely means "I" as opposed to any specific part of one's anatomy. Chan was also used when addressing superiors with whom you were familiar.

Another word which definitely means "I" is *ku* – now considered impolite but used by King Ramkhamhaeng the Great (13th Century) almost throughout his stone inscriptions.

So the picture emerges of the highest part of one's own person addressing the lowest part of the other person. And the higher in rank or status the other person is, the more the lowest part is accentuated.

To make this picture even more complete, it would, I think, perhaps be suitable to add what I mentioned in Chapter 1 when dealing with *rachasap* – the Royal Language; when addressing supreme royalty, that is to say, Their Majesties the King or Queen, the correct mode of address *is taifala-*

*ong thuliphra baht* – literally, "coarse visible dust, fine invisible dust, under soles of gracious feet." This is because the sovereign has always been considered as standing so high above others that he cannot be addressed directly; even his feet are above the eye-level of ordinary people, so one must address the dust *beneath* the soles of his feet. (But as all the world knows, this does not prevent the great warmth and affection that exist between Their Majesties and their people, and the frequent informal conversations which Their Majesties have with people in all walks of life, especially upcountry).

I would like to add one final remark about the expression M.R. Ayumongol used in his column – *tok rong*. I cannot find this in So Sethaputra's *New Model Thai-English Dictionary*. The nearest translation I can arrive at is "stuck in a groove" – like a needle in an old-fashioned gramophone record that keeps on playing the same thing over and over again. This expression may have originated, I am told, in the 1920s or 1930s when gramophone needles were much heavier affairs than today. But the literal translation "stuck in a groove" does not, I think, convey the correct meaning of *tok rong*. I think a much nearer approximation would be "having a bee in one's bonnet," or, as the French say, an *idée fixé*.

Now for another topic, suggested by an English colleague in the office. "Have you ever thought about the Thai words for things which are not native to Thailand?" he asked. He gave me a few random examples which had occurred to him: A satellite (man-made), *dao thiam* (literally, "artificial star"); television, *thorathat*; darts, *luk dok* ("child of a flower", which I mentioned earlier); kangaroo, *ching-cho*, and snow – definitely not native to Thailand – *hima*.

My comments on those examples are that the first one

234

seems fairly obvious; Thai is essentially a pragmatic language, and the fine distinction between a star and a satellite is probably considered an unnecessary refinement. Television I will return to that in a minute, because this kind of word is in a special class. Why a dart should be the child of a flower I have no idea (nor have Thai friends whom I have asked); nor can I tell you anything about *ching-cho* except that it seems a suitably suggestive word for an animal that leaps up and down (like a yo-yo, perhaps?); *hima*, snow, obviously has its origin in the Himalayas, for which the Thai name is *himawan*, "a snow-covered region or forest."

The English word "television" comes from the ancient Greek root *tele-* meaning "far," and the Latin *visionem*, "sight." And in just the same way, the Thai word *thorathat* comes from two Sanskrit roots: *Tora*, also meaning "far," and *tat*, also meaning "sight." In fact the Greek *tele-* and the Sanskrit *thora-* are themselves related to each other, both coming from the much older Indo-European family of languages.

The significance and interest of "television" and its Thai counterpart *thoratat* is that both of them are new words expressing modern ideas by means of ancient classical root-words. In the same group of words are telephone, *thorasap*, and telegram, *thoralek*, the similarities between English and Thai are for the same reason.

We can also add the Thai word for "automatic," which has an uncannily similar sound: *attanomat*. The first time I came across this word, I thought it was a straight adaptation from the English word; but it is not. The Sanskrit for "self" is *atrnan*, and the Pali is *atta*: the Greek is *auto-*. See what I mean?

But there are also a few fairly new words which have been adapted into Thai straight from English (and I am not thinking of "football"!). One of them is *samana*, a seminar – a very fashionable word these days in education, business, and public relations. Another is *sathi-ti*. Any guesses what that means? Statistics!

There are also a few new and strange Thai words such as *samongkon*, a computer. (*Samong* means "brain" and *kon* means "machinery"). This word is too new even to be in the dictionary. Another new word (which is in the dictionary) is *samo-son*, a society or club. Although new, it is taken from Pali word.

To end with, a word which has always interests me is the Thai for electricity, *fai-fa*, literally "sky-fire." Recently I was reading a book about King Mongkut. One day during his long period in the monkhood before ascending the throne, Mongkut and a fellow-monk visited an American friend who was fond of dabbling in scientific experiments. He showed the two monks and a crowd of curious onlookers how an electric current could be produced. Everyone was amazed, and called it "fire from the sky." Is that, perhaps how the modern Thai word originated?

# CHAPTER TEN
# Miscellaneous

## Phra Pathom *Chedi*

Phra Pathom *Chedi*, the huge pagoda at Nakhon Pathom some thirty-five miles west of Bangkok, was in the news quite a number of years ago because of the restoration work going on to repair the cracks in it.

The name "Phra Pathom Chedi" means literally "the holy first pagoda," and Nakhon Pathom means "the first city." The word *pathom* comes from the same root as *prathom*, although the two words are spelt differently in Thai. Both words mean "first," but *prathom* is used in the sense of elementary or primary education as opposed to secondary education.

Nakhon Pathom, "the first city," was so called because there is a considerable amount of historical and archaeological evidence indicating that this is the place where Buddhism first took root in Thailand, and Phra Pathom Chedi is believed to be the most ancient Buddhist pagoda in the country. It is said that the Emperor Asoka of India, a devout Buddhist, sent out two missionaries, Sona and Uttara, by ship about twenty-two hundred years ago to a region then known as "Suvarnabhumi" (pronounced "Suwanapoom"), which means "the Golden Land" and which corresponded roughly to Southeast Asia. Local archaeological findings have suggested that these two Buddhist emissaries landed at the spot where Nakhon Pathom now stands. (At that time it was on the coast, because the level of the Gulf of Thailand was higher than it is today.) The location was not then in the country we know as Thailand; it was part of the Mon Kingdom of Dvaravati. It was not to become part of Siam or Thailand for another fifteen hundred years or more.

The *chedi*, or pagoda, which marks this historic spot has, in the words of Professor Frank E. Reynolds of the University of Chicago in a lecture given to the Siam Society in February 1974, "a long and illustrious tradition behind it. Both in the pre-Thai period and in the history of the later Thai kingdoms, this famous *chedi* has been rebuilt and enlarged on a number of different occasions. It received basically its present form through the repair and reconstruction efforts encouraged by King Mongkut (Rama IV) in the latter half of the nineteenth century, and from that time forward it has been one of the most sacred and visited shrines in all of Thailand."

King Mongkut, in fact, having seen the old, original 130-foot-high structure which is believed to date back about sixteen hundred years, wanted to restore it. But this proved impossible owing to its poor state of preservation. Instead, he built an enormous bowl-shaped dome over the old *chedi*, completely enclosing it. His son, King Chulalongkorn (Rama V), completed the work about hundred years or so ago. It is this huge dome, covered with glazed copper-colored tiles brought by King Chulalongkorn from China, which one sees today. It stands 413 feet high, dominating the town of Nakhon Pathom and the surrounding countryside; it is the biggest Buddhist structure in Thailand and probably in the whole world. Visitors come in their tens of thousands every year, especially during November when there is a temple fair lasting three days.

Since my first visit to Phra Pathom Chedi in 1965, I have been back to visit the beautiful pagoda several times.

Inside the compound are small exquisitely shaped belfries from which sweet-toned bells ring out every so often. At the four points of the compass in the outer courtyard are four *wihan*, or small chapels, each containing a Buddha image in a different posture.

Professor Reynolds had some interesting things to say about the postures of these four images during his lecture to the Siam Society. A *chedi*, he says, is a symbol both of the Buddha's career, which culminated in his reaching Nirvana, and of the continuing effect of his power and message in the life of the Buddhist community. So it is not surprising that the Phra Pathom *Chedi* includes representations of important events in the Master's life. The eastern *wihan*, or chapel, contains an image representing the moment of the Buddha's Great Awakening, or Enlightenment, under the Bo tree at Bodh Gaya in India. The delicately painted Bo tree covers the entire wall behind the image. Proceeding in a clockwise direction round the *chedi*, the Buddha's life-story continues in the south chapel with the Master preaching his first sermon in the Deer Park at Benares. In the western chapel, a great reclining Buddha shows the Master just before his death and attainment of Nirvana.

Then why is the fourth figure, on the north side, a standing one? And why is it specially venerated by the Thai people?

Professor Reynolds answers these questions by pointing out three facts. First, this standing image is known as Phra Ruang Rochanarit, a popular name for the kings of the Sukhothai Kingdom, to whom the Thais have traditionally looked as national founders and supporters of Buddhism. Secondly, the head of this image was originally attached to an image of the Sukhothai period, perhaps a portrait statue commissioned by one of the later members of the Ruang Dynasty to represent himself and the Buddha in a single image. Finally, the base of the present statue contains the ashes of the king who commissioned it and had it installed at Phra Pathom *Chedi*: King Vajiravudh or Rama VI. From these three facts Professor Reynolds concludes that this image represents the continuation of the Buddha's work, after he reached Nirvana, through the agency of the Thai kings, and the establishment of the Buddhist faith as a basic part of the life of the Thai nation.

It was on another visit to the Phra Pathom Chedi that I was first shown the many small *chedi* made of sand in the temple compound, looking like elongated children's sandcastles decorated with faded garlands of flowers. These sand *chedi* are usually built by the faithful around the time of *Songkran* Day, the ancient Thai New Year in mid-April. Upcountry, such *chedi* are sometimes made both within the grounds of the temple and on the village meeting ground. A Thai friend tells me he has heard one theory that the purpose of building these miniature *chedi* inside the temple grounds once a year is to replace all the sand belonging to the temple which one has inadvertently carried away on the soles and heels of one's shoes in the course of the year!

Phra Pathom *Chedi* was never in any danger of toppling over. However, cracks had developed in the dome beneath the tiles as well as other structural damage over the years. The Government provided about 35 million baht for repairs, which were completed in the early 1980s, and we can once more take delight in the magnificent copper-gold *chedi* in "the first city."

# An Unexpected English Lesson

I once met four senior schoolboys from Nakhon Si Thammarat in the South of Thailand. Our acquaintance was all too short, but I would like to write about it. I had gone back to spend a week (as a layman) at the temple where I was ordained as a monk a year previously – Wat Chonprathan, opposite the Irrigation Department near Nonthaburi, just north of Bangkok. The abbot arranged for the elderly monk who looks after the *kuti*'s (monk's dwellings) to supply me with breakfast every morning, and this was how I got to know his four *luk-sit*, or temple attendants.

At first I thought the four boys were the old monk's regular attendants. But then, after they had brought me my breakfast a couple of mornings, they told me something which I found very interesting and typical of Thailand.

They said they were students from Nakhon Si Thammarat, 700 miles south of Bangkok, who had passed their M.S. 5 (school-leaving) exams and had come to Bangkok to sit for the university entrance examination. Now normally when people have to come to Bangkok from the provinces, they stay with relatives or friends; but these four boys had no one in Bangkok with whom they could stay. So they chose to stay at the temple, "working their passage" by washing dishes and doing all the other chores for the elderly monk in return for free lodging. They had to do some of their chores early in the morning before setting off by bus for Bangkok and their daily exams, which I think went on for about two weeks, and finish off the rest of the dishwashing and other jobs when they got back again in the evening.

This dependence on the temple is simply a continuation of the centuries-old Thai tradition whereby all travelers of old stayed as a matter of general practice at the local temple.

It is just one more facet illustrating the deep and important role which the temples of this country still play in the nation's social life.

Can you guess what's coming? Well, among their exam subjects the boys had to take two, three-hour English papers . . . So not unnaturally, early one morning one of the boys shyly approached me as I was sitting on the verandah of the *kuti*. He had a book of old exam papers, mostly what are known in educational circles as "multiple-choice questions" ("State which answer, a, b, c, or d, you consider best fits the question"). The boy himself had just two questions to put to me: (a) Was I either American or English, and (b) If so, would I please help him? I said I was English. Before I had a chance to say "yes" to his second question, he was quickly joined by his three pals who crowded round the small space on the verandah, just as eager as he was to improve their English.

In fact, I discovered right way that they could understand me quite well in English and they had a respectable working knowledge of the language, though I had some difficulty in understanding them because of their incorrect stressing and pronunciation. This was quite excusable and normal especially with people from the provinces, because they probably never had a chance to speak English with a native English speaker in their entire lives.

Anyway, they asked me to tell them which out of the four alternative choices was the correct answers to each question. But this I flatly refused to do. "No, YOU tell ME!" I said sternly, at which they all burst out laughing.

They managed to get most of the answers right. When they were wrong, they didn't just leave it at that, but insisted on knowing why they were wrong. That is what I like – not just simple acceptance of what I say, but a desire to really try to understand the working of our often tortuous and utterly illogical language. (Have you ever tried counting how many verb tenses there are In English? I did, once; I think it is eleven or twelve!)

And so we went on for nearly two hours, during which we all laughed a lot. The day after that they were tied up with their geography exam, and then there was no more time left. But just before sunset on the day of the English exam I sat outside the old monk's *kuti*, my ankles bitten to bits by mosquitoes, checking over the boys' results with them. They seemed to have done quite well, and I feel reasonably sure all four boys passed the entrance exam and were able to go on to university. (I think one of them said he wanted to study medicine at Mahidol University, another wanted to do agriculture at Kasetsat, and a third was planning on Political Science at Chulalongkorn University).

I never really got to know these boys well enough to find out their names. But I know that these four youngsters from Nakhon Si Thammarat will become good and useful citizens, examples to whatever foreign countries they may visit of all that is best in the Thai people.

DENIS SEGALLER was born in London in 1915. As a child, he was taken all over Europe by his parents and went to school in Switzerland. Later his career as a documentary filmmaker again often took him on trips overseas, however he never visited Asia until his work brought him to Thailand in 1965.

Like many Englishmen, he eventually grew so fond of Thailand that he decided to make it his permanent home. He married a Thai, switched careers to that of a newspaper writer at the age of fifty-nine, and soon afterwards, somewhat to his surprise, suddenly became a Buddhist.

Many Thai traditions and customs are very different from those of other countries, especially in the West – a fact which makes them of great interest to non-Thais, and to westerners in particular. Yet often enough, if one digs a bit deeper, it can be seen that the differences are not as great as they appear on the surface; all of us, non-Thais and Thais alike, are very much the same human beings under the skin.

The collection of articles in this book gives the non-Thai reader some insight into the delightful people of Thailand, how they live, and how they react to life's varied situations, as seen through the eyes of an Englishman who many years ago made Thailand his permanent home.